The Just-Right Challenge

9 Strategies *to Ensure Adolescents* **Don't Drop Out** *of the Game*

Stevi Quate | John McDermott

HEINEMANN
Portsmouth, NH

Heinemann
361 Hanover Street
Portsmouth, NH 03801–3912
www.heinemann.com

Offices and agents throughout the world

The authors and publisher wish to thank those who have generously given permission to reprint borrowed material:

Figure Intro 1: "Challenge Skills Match" from *Finding Flow* by Mihaly Csikszentmihalyi. Copyright © 1997 by Mihaly Csikszentmihalyi. Published by Basic Books, a Member of the Perseus Books Group. Reprinted by permission of the publisher via the Copyright Clearance Center, www.copyright.com.

Figure 5.5: "Emotional Safety" from *Relationship-Driven Classroom Management* by John M. Vitto. Copyright © 2003. Published by Sage Publications, Inc. Reprinted by permission of the publisher via the Copyright Clearance Center, www.copyright.com.

Library of Congress Cataloging-in-Publication Data
Quate, Stevi.
  The just-right challenge : 9 strategies to ensure adolescents don't drop out of the game / Stevi Quate and John McDermott.
      pages   cm
  Includes bibliographical references and index.
  ISBN 978-0-325-04902-1
1. Achievement motivation. 2. Teenagers—Education. 3. Dropouts—Prevention. I. McDermott, John. II. Title.
  LB1065.Q38 2013
  370.15'4—dc23   2013008010

Editor: Samantha Bennett
Production editor: Sonja S. Chapman
Typesetter: Kim Arney
Cover and interior designs: Suzanne Heiser
Manufacturing: Steve Bernier

Printed in the United States of America on acid-free paper
17   16   15   14   13   VP   1   2   3   4   5

Dedication

To Victoria Soto, Dawn Lafferty Hochsprung, Lauren Rousseau, Mary Sherlach, Rachel D'Avino, Anne Marie Murphy, and William Sanders. They are the heart of teaching.

—*John*

To my son, Dean, who taught me about tackling the "just-right challenge" and challenges that were monumental. You persevered with a great spirit, and I love you.

—*Stevi*

Contents

Foreword

When a disheartened, disengaged student, working with a dedicated teacher, becomes a motivated, engaged learner, the results can be breathtaking. But making that transformation happen is, of course, not a simple matter.

In *The Just-Right Challenge: 9 Strategies to Ensure Adolescents Don't Drop Out of the Game*, Stevi Quate and John McDermott take us into the classrooms of teachers who seem to "create magic." They reveal, with compelling clarity, a set of approaches and practices that highly effective teachers use to "engage students in doing important, relevant, challenging, intellectual work."

With concrete strategies and classroom success stories, the authors illustrate the importance of adopting a teaching stance that promotes in students what education researcher Carol Dweck calls a "growth mindset"—the belief that an individual can "grow their smartness" through determination and hard work. Quate and McDermott speak persuasively about bringing authenticity into the classroom to engage students with ideas they will find relevant—while teaching the critical thinking and subject matter students need to master. And they discuss methods for providing students of all learning levels access to challenging material.

Far too many students drop out of school each year—one every 26 seconds. I know I am not alone in saying that an effective, quality education for all is the economic, moral, and civil rights imperative of our time. It is absolutely critical that we work together to help more students meet their potential. And with schools throughout the country taking on the Common Core State Standards that focus on ensuring students have the skills and knowledge to succeed in a twenty-first-century economy, *The Just-Right Challenge* is a particularly timely resource for teachers who are on the front lines of the dropout crisis and America's urban education challenge.

As cofounder and CEO of City Year, an education-focused non-profit that harnesses the power of young people in national service to help keep students in school and on track to graduation, I have the opportunity to get to know many inspirational City Year AmeriCorps members. Using our "Whole School, Whole Child" service model that focuses holistically on students' academic and social-emotional development, our corps members dedicate a year of their lives to serve alongside teachers in high-poverty schools in 25 cities nationwide.

Each year I hear from more corps members, especially those who have been inspired by working with a particularly talented and passionate teacher, who finish their year of service and decide to become teachers themselves. They feel driven to continue to help students "get in the game," a mission Quate and McDermott write about so powerfully in the pages that follow. I know that these young teachers, as well as seasoned classroom veterans, will benefit tremendously from reading *The Just-Right Challenge*, and incorporating its principles into their teaching practice.

Whether you are a teacher, education leader, or simply a concerned and thoughtful person looking for "what works" in public education, this important book has vital lessons for us all.

—Michael Brown

Acknowledgments

After *Clock Watchers* was written, several teachers we met at a conference talked to us about challenge. Oh, yes, they believed in challenging their students, but they wrestled with how to challenge all their students appropriately. They knew what to do with students in the college track, but struggled with figuring out the "just-right" challenge for other students. We listened, commiserated with them, and offered some ideas, but we knew we had to get smarter about challenge.

At the same time, we were spending more and more time in urban schools and saw teachers confronting the realities of teaching students whose lives are filled with unbelievable difficulties. Some teachers worried about adding stress to their students' lives and offered their students simple, easy work while others shook their heads in frustration because so many of their kids were failing. What could they do, they asked time and time again, to engage their students in learning, especially when skills were low? We needed to give them answers and offer them hope.

Several of the schools where we worked were deemed low performing because of the scores on the state assessments. One school where John worked began the process of being reconstituted because of those low scores. Many of the teachers were demoralized and many felt close to giving up in defeat. Yet several teachers still new in the profession continued challenging their students and

watching them grow. These teachers inspired us and motivated us to continue looking hard at the concept of challenge.

For several years, we closely studied teachers as they wrestled with the all the demands of the profession yet, often, managed to create the conditions that would challenge, motivate, and engage their students. Sometimes they admitted defeat, but they always picked themselves up and moved forward, figuring out what they could do next.

Without those teachers who graciously opened their doors for us to come and watch them teach, this book couldn't have been written. To Kathy Cocetti, Lesli Cochran, Pat Jackson, Antwan Jefferson, Kim Kern, Steve Lash, Sherry Long, Ryan Martine, Sue Martino, Negar Mizani, Jennifer Reinert, Kathy Sampson, Emily Skrobko, Martha Tudor, and Alisa Wills-Keely, thank you all!

Without the stories from our students, our book would not have included the voices of those who matter, so thank you to Justin Cochran, Connor Kimpel, Jerardo, Jacquelyn Villa, June Robles, and all the other students who let us sit next to them and eavesdrop.

We have to thank the Public Education and Business Coalition (PEBC) for all its work with teachers across the nation. If it weren't for the PEBC, we would not have been able to spend time in classrooms across the nation, working side by side with teachers and collaborating to make their classrooms a place where we would all like to linger. In particular, thank you to Paula Miller for believing in our work; to Annie Patterson for asking hard questions and believing we might have some answers; and to Wendy Hoffer-Ward for being such an inspiration as you challenged teachers to be the kind of thinkers you knew they were.

Special thanks to our editor, Sam Bennett, who believed that we could really pull it together and write the story that needed to be told. And, finally, we want to acknowledge those wonderful people in our lives who listened to us talk one more time about our book, who waited for us as we pounded out one more chapter, and who patiently gave us the gift of time as we thought, read, and wrestled with ideas:

- For John: My wife, Pat, who is my life; my daughters, Katie and Maggie, who inspire me; and my sons-in-law, Matt and Zach, who bring joy into our family.
- For Stevi: My husband, Jim, who once again believed in my work; and my son, Dean, my daughter-in-law, Theresa, and my grandchildren, Connor and Cali, who keep me going!

Here's to the teachers who give their all for the learning and growth of others.

If I am through learning, I am through.

—John Wooden

Getting in the Game

Stevi and the Game

Today in my Body Pump class, I noticed a T-shirt that read "Get in the Game." Even though I was the oldest one in the class, I was still pumping that weight and lifting more than classmates much younger than I. I thought about how I love the game of exercise. In a good class, on a good bike ride, or on a mountain hike, I lose track of time and concentrate on the moment. I am in the state of flow.

Who would have thought that I would be curious about a clean and press? Who would have thought that a kickback would be a kick in the butt for me? The longer I was in the Body Pump class, the more skills I developed, the more weight I could handle, and the prouder I was of being in my sixties and knowing how to load weight onto the bar.

I was in the game.

John and the Game

Recently, my daughter Maggie and I had a conversation about the California Bar Exam that she had just completed. For Maggie, the three-day exam was an exhilarating experience. "For the first time in my educational career I was challenged in a way that forced me to use all my skills. I enjoyed the opportunity to engage in this demonstration of my learning." The smile on Maggie's face told the story; after nineteen years of schooling, she finally was given a task that matched her skills.

Maggie enjoyed the game.

Students and the Game

And that's what we want for all our students: to be in the game of learning. To be fully engaged in getting smarter and smarter.

Connor

Connor, too, wanted to be in that game—that is, up until a few years ago. Like many young boys, he arrived at school eager to learn and excited about playing the big-boy role of kindergartner. But by the end of fourth grade, his enthusiasm had drifted away, and by seventh grade, he clearly couldn't care less about the school game. What he had learned was that he wasn't particularly good in that role. But get him on the basketball court, and he'd be in *that* game. He practiced hours and hours alone and with buddies, and when game time came he was fully engaged and having a great time. As the years went by, he ceased practicing the game of school at home altogether unless his parents were standing over him. He pulled back from reading and writing and plunged into a serious decline. One ray of hope, though, was when he discovered *Diary of a Wimpy Kid*. All his buddies were reading the book and making jokes about farting and burping, just like Greg in the book. But at about the same time that Connor was burping like Greg, he was assigned *The Good Earth* by Pearl Buck, a novel appropriate for high school seniors or college students.

The school Connor was attending prided itself on being challenging. No intellectual wimps there. In fact, the motto of the school read: *An engaging place where students achieve and thrive in a challenging liberal arts program.* For Connor, the last part of the statement was true: it was truly a challenging program; however, it was not the place for him to achieve or to thrive. Instead, the challenges that the school prided itself on were over the top for him and resulted in his nonengagement.

Justin

Down the road, Justin was engaged in the game of school, but it was not the same game that the school had intended. Instead, Justin and his friends, all reputed to be the school's best scholars, made a deal with each other: who could maintain that straight A record but have the lowest A possible? To play this version of the school game, Justin checked his grades nightly, noting how close he was to a B. Based on what he learned, he would reflect on his assigned homework. Busy work? If the answer was yes, he'd do it only if he needed it to maintain that A. Otherwise, afternoons were for sports and nights were for getting smarter about music theory, an area of personal passion.

During the school day, he'd do his second-period homework during first period, third-period homework during second period, and so on throughout the day. He explained that teachers primarily lectured, so it was easy for him to fake attention on the lecture and look like he was taking notes, when in truth, he was concentrating on homework from a completely different class. Justin understood and applied the rules of the game with ease, but he needed a more challenging league.

Justin, by the way, finished his high school career with straight As and was awarded a very prestigious scholarship. In fact, he graduated a year early. He was definitely a winner at playing the game of school, even if his version of the game wasn't shared by others.

Jerardo

But there's another story about getting in the game of school. This is the story of Jerardo, who never thought that he would play this game, let alone be successful at it. School had always been difficult and his life at home was a mess. His parents didn't value school and wrestled with financial and legal issues. He attended school only because of a court mandate, not out of passion and definitely not out of a desire to be in the game. But in one year things shifted for him. In his humanities class, he discovered novels about students who looked like him and who loved the sports that he loved. Jerardo read his first novel there and then his second and then his third. One day in science class, he thought he was safe reading his novel tucked inside the fat science textbook. Lost in his book, he didn't hear his teacher coming up behind him. When the teacher scolded him for reading and not listening, Jerardo knew that he was changing—and so did his friends, who teased him about being a school boy—but he didn't care. He was learning the rules of the game and he wanted to play.

Connor, Justin, and Jerardo all represent what this book is about: how schools can create the context that motivates and engages students and that challenges them just enough so that they want to be players in the game of school instead of sitting on a bench daydreaming about personal passions. We know that too much challenge can send kids like Connor intellectually and emotionally out of the game, and too little challenge can result in students creating their own version of the game, like Justin. But we also know that some students, like Jerardo, are challenged and become engaged in school. The questions we asked as we wrote this book were: *What does it look and sound like when challenge motivates and engages students? What does a teacher do to make challenge work? And what about students in our urban schools? How do we engage them through challenge?*

Why the Urgency?

Not only is providing all students challenging intellectual work the ethical thing to do but the political climate demands it for all students. With the Common Core State Standards (CCSS), challenge isn't an option. In the introduction to the standards, the insistence on challenge is made clear: "Promoting a culture of high expectations for all students is a fundamental goal of the common core state standards" (Common Core State Standards Initiative 2010, 6). These standards have rigor and challenge embedded in each standard.

In fact, the CCSS insist that all students, including English language learners and students with disabilities, have a right to be held to the same high expectations. No longer is a challenging curriculum reserved for students in the upper academic tracks; it's a requirement for all. What changes are the appropriate instructional supports and the amount of time needed for each of the standards.

> The National Governors Association Center for Best Practices and the Council of Chief State School Officers strongly believe that all students should be held to the same high expectations outlined in the Common Core State Standards. This includes students who are English language learners (ELLs). However, these students may require additional time, appropriate instructional support, and aligned assessments as they acquire both English language proficiency and content area knowledge. (Common Core State Standards Initiative 2012a)

The same conditions hold for students with disabilities:

> All students, including students with disabilities—students eligible under the Individuals with Disabilities Education Act (IDEA)—must be challenged to excel within the general curriculum and prepared for success in their post-school lives, including college and or careers. The common score state standards provide a historic opportunity to improve access to academic content standards for students with disabilities. . . . Therefore, how these high standards are taught and assessed is of the utmost importance in reaching this diverse group of students. (Common Core State Standards Initiative 2012b)

Advocates of the Common Core State Standards often note how these standards reflect the twenty-first-century skills students need to succeed in the future. Those skills include critical thinking and problem solving, certainly two important elements of challenge. The Four Cs of 21st Century Skills begin with "critical thinking," defined as "problem-solving, research, analysis, project management, etc." (Partnership for 21st Century Skills). This call for students to do work that is challenging is based on today's needs as well as those of the future. In *The Highly Engaged Classroom*, Marzano and Pickering argue that the jobs of today and the future require workers who can conquer cognitively demanding tasks: "Tasks that require use of cognitively challenging skills are not simply engaging then, they are essential" (2011, 15).

Why Challenge? Why Not Rigor?

Clearly, this notion of challenge is prevalent in educational circles. But often it's couched in the language of *rigor*. Not quite comfortable with that word, we turned to our colleagues to find out what the buzz was about. One educator, twenty-five years into the profession, snickered, "It's the latest buzz word. I wonder what that word will be next year."

Kathy, an English teacher, shook her head and said, "The sad thing is that I expect my students to produce excellent essays, and I work with them until they get there. I can tell this pays off in a thousand ways including on the state assessment since my students' scores are always strong and some of the best in our school. However, my administration doesn't think I'm rigorous enough because I insist students rewrite and rewrite some more until their work hits the mark. They think I'm being too easy by allowing students to rewrite until they get their work right. Plus because I don't have tons of grades in my gradebook, my administrators question rigor in my classes."

Another teacher, much younger and with only five years of teaching experience, commented, "I'm still not sure what it means to be rigorous. Wish someone would help me figure out how I can tell—unless it's about watching how much agony I can see on my students' faces."

Curious about the dictionary definition of *rigor*, we turned to Merriam-Webster and found the following: 1 a (1): harsh inflexibility in opinion, temper, or judgment : severity (2) : the quality of being unyielding or inflexible : strictness (3) : severity of life : austerity b : an act or instance of strictness, severity, or cruelty (www.merriam-webster.com/dictionary/rigor).

These definitions didn't work for us. Worried about the cynicism that we heard from our colleagues, we turned away from the word *rigor* and returned to our framework for motivating and engaging students that we explored in *Clock Watchers* (Quate and Mc-Dermott 2009): challenge. Again we turn to Merriam-Webster and found this definition of challenge: a stimulating task or problem (www.merriam-webster.com/dictionary/challenge). This definition worked for us. We agree with Joan Wink, who says, "To understand rigor in schools today . . ., think rigor mortis . . . [We need] more vigor and less rigor" (2011, 38). So *rigor* was certainly not the term we were after, but *challenge* was. True, the terms often are intended to be interchangeable, but rigor carries connotations that we wanted to avoid while challenge captured our hope for engaging, vigorous, stimulating instruction. After all, we thought, it wasn't rigor that enticed Stevi into the exercise game nor was it rigor that engaged John's daughter. It was challenge.

But What Is Challenge?

We're defining challenge as stimulating intellectual work that is toward the end of a student's zone of proximal development, demanding effort and requiring depth of knowledge. The problem, of course, is that challenge varies from student to student and, as a result, requires a teacher to know her students well in order to provide that "just-right" level of challenge.

As we perused the research and reflected on the teachers we describe in this book, we learned that challenge that engages can be understood through three lenses: the stance of the teacher, the nature of the academic work, and student access.

Teaching Stance

A teacher's stance matters. But what is stance and why is it important? Under the umbrella of a teaching stance, you'll find a teacher's beliefs about students and learning, attitude toward the profession, and opinions on educational issues and practices. Stance refers to how a teacher positions herself in relationship to teaching, learning, curriculum, instruction, and even assessment and grading. It's an encapsulation of the beliefs, attitudes, and philosophical positions that prop up the moves that a teacher makes. Stance is revealed through how a teacher orchestrates lesson plans, uses time in the classroom, answers questions, decorates and arranges her room, and provides the scaffolds necessary for success. Each of these concrete practices provides a window into her beliefs and reveals her stance.

For all students to do difficult, challenging work, a teacher must take the stand that all students can learn, even those who come from poverty, those with unique learning needs, and those who have historically been disenfranchised by the system. The teaching stance must include the unflinching belief that each student walks into the classroom with strengths and funds of knowledge (Moll et al. 2001). It is up to that teacher to learn about the local community and the culture and background of her students in order to understand the funds they bring with them and then to build from that knowledge. Such a teacher believes that students come into the classroom with a myriad of assets that can be infused into the curriculum, that students can get smarter, and that the teacher's role is to scaffold learning and then to remove those scaffolds.

Tomlinson and Imbeau (2011) capture the way in which a teacher's beliefs shape basic classroom decision making:

> When teachers are afraid of what might happen when students work independently, in small groups, with inquiry-oriented tasks, or at varied paces, they often opt to use more passive approaches to learning that effectually "dumb down" the curriculum. In those instances, teachers lower their expectations for students by using simpler modes of presentation and evaluation as a trade-off for classroom order. In other words, in those circumstances, teachers "teach defensively." (77)

As Tomlinson and Imbeau imply, the way teachers use the precious commodity of time often depends on where the teacher stands on who should be doing the talking, the problem solving, the reading, or the thinking. If a teacher's stance is focused on her expertise, she is more likely to structure time so that she is doing the majority of the intellectual heavy lifting. However, a teacher who recognizes the funds of knowledge students bring with them is likely to use that commodity of time in a way that allows students to be, as Ted Sizer said years ago, the workers in the classroom (2004).

A teaching stance must include an unwavering commitment to the power of education to transform society. Joan Wink, in *Critical Pedagogy* (2011), helps us think about this grander purpose when she states that education needs to be about transformation. Not only should the work stretch the student's ability but it should also help the learner get better at doing work that matters in their world. If education is to transform students, then a teacher must work from a sense of urgency and agency.

The Nature of the Academic Work

On occasion teachers err on the side of easy, thinking that if students can be successful performing an easy task then they will be motivated to do tougher work. However, the opposite appears to be true (Csikszentmihalyi 2008; Marzano and Pickering 2011). Work that requires students to dig in and wrestle with ideas actually has more staying power than easy work. Work that challenges and engages is complex, requiring critical thinking.

Students need work with an *academic press*—a sense of "press" to engage in academic challenge in a teacher-designed environment—that demands they think at a cognitively high level on important issues. A teacher in Kentucky, Pat Jackson, upped the challenge of a unit by increasing the complexity of the task and fueled the students' engagement. Her goals were to develop the skills of her middle school students as readers of nonfiction and as writers of solid arguments. To work toward those goals, she posed an essential question: Is it ethical for people to have wild animals as pets?

The first year that she taught the unit, she gave students articles to read about a chimp that ripped the face off its owner's best friend. Those articles led students to one answer: of course, it was wrong to keep a wild animal as a pet. The second year, she moved her students to analyze, interpret, and evaluate multiple viewpoints. She brought in articles with different perspectives, including the story of a man who raised a cheetah from a cub to an adult and saved its life. That cheetah then became an important part of the scientific community. By intentionally going after ambiguity, Pat increased the challenge and heightened student engagement.

Another element of engaging work that is challenging is that it is authentic and reflects the world outside of school (Newmann 1992). When students see that what they are doing is not just work done in school but work that matches the real world, the task has the potential of hooking them. Jeff Wilhelm (2007) refers to this match as the correspondence concept: work that corresponds to the work that experts in the field do. Recently Stevi read a blog entry that exemplifies this concept. A teacher learned about an upcoming conference and invited her students to create a similar conference within their school. In the process, her students interviewed the scientists who attended the other conference and actually participated in conversations with them.

Authentic work is important, but the work must also be culturally relevant and transformative. As Freire and Macedo (1987) state, we must teach our children to read the world as well as the word. Work that is culturally relevant allows students to connect learning to their personal experiences, school experiences, and local community experiences. This is an education with the power to transform society and the individual. As teachers plan ways to challenge students, they must intentionally include either the students' personal, school, or community context into instruction. In an upcoming chapter you'll read about Jennifer Reinert, a high school math teacher who challenged her class to consider the statistics of race and high school suspensions and calculate the probability that the students sitting in her class would be suspended. This is not only authentic work; it allows students to investigate their school community through the lens of social justice and equity. Whenever a teacher connects academic work to its context in the real world, she is positioning it to be culturally relevant and challenging *and engaging*.

Student Access

Mihaly Csikszentmihalyi (pronounced chick-sent-me-high-ee) is a Hungarian psychologist who spent his life studying happiness and was awarded Thinker of the Year in 2000. We embraced his theory of flow in our first book, *Clock Watchers*. Capturing the state of engagement that we were after, Csikszentmihalyi (1997, 2008) described flow as those moments when we're immersed in an experience and lose track of time, those times when our concentration is matched by enjoyment and a high sense of interest. We wanted *engagement* to mean more to students than being actively involved in the learning; we wanted them to feel what happens when intellectually hooked by an academic experience.

In his research, Csikszentmihalyi found an interesting pattern for flow experiences or those optimal learning experiences. When a person's skill set and the level of challenge match, the person is set for flow. However, when there's a mismatch, other emotions set in (see Figure I.1).

Think about Connor for a minute. Connor's skills were low for the tasks he was being asked to do: challenges high and skills low. As a result, he meandered back and forth between anxiety and boredom and ended up refusing to play. After being highly anxious that he couldn't succeed, he often would shut down intellectually. Justin, on the other hand, had very high skills, but the work offered little challenge. He approached his high school career from an extremely relaxed perspective, knowing that he could

Figure I.1: Challenge Skills Match

The quality of experience as a function of the relationship between challenges and skills. Optimal experience, or flow, occurs when both variables are high.

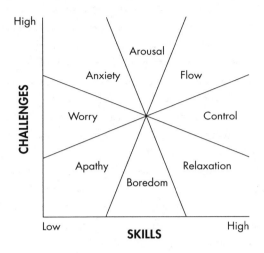

Sources: Adapted from Massimini and Carli 1988: Csikszentmihalyi 1990; 1997.

maintain his A with minimum effort. Justin needed a game that matched his skills. Jerardo, too, is reflected on Csikszentmihalyi's chart. At first, his skills in reading were quite low, but as he developed more expertise and gained a sense of control, he looked forward to reading another novel and frequently found himself in that state of flow. In addition, Jerardo saw the connection of the work he was doing to his life. In the past, school work seemed disconnected from this life, and even though teachers claimed the work was relevant, he didn't believe it. For him, and or many students like him, it was important to be able to name how the work was relevant to his life.

Vygotsky's (1989) work on the zone of proximal development (ZPD) also informs our work. Very simply, the ZPD can be illustrated by learning to ride a bicycle. The ZPD ranges from the early days of learning to ride when a young bicyclist needs training wheels to the time when he can hop on the bike and ride with confidence and skill. Vygotsky stressed the social component of learning. We learn from him how the influence of mentors, peers, and more knowledgeable others can grow students. So as students become more skilled as intellectuals, they need to work and learn within a community.

Our argument is that teachers can provide students a way to access challenging work that is just beyond their current skill level. To do this, though, teachers are wise to consider Carol Dweck's (2006) research on mindset. Dweck contrasts two mindsets, fixed and growth, and shows how mindsets shape students' willingness to exert the intellectual effort to complete a task. Learners who see their ability and intelligence as fixed—either they're born smart or they're born dumb—resist engaging in work that threatens their view of themselves or that requires a skill set they don't have and don't believe they can get. In contrast, students with a growth mindset, who see that they can grow smartness by cultivating the intellectual tools they need to be successful, are more likely to get in the game. Jerardo, like other students we'll describe, shifted from a fixed to a growth mindset. We'll watch what happens to them in upcoming chapters and see how their teachers were able to show them that they could become smart and capable of doing hard work and they deserved that chance.

Laura Viergutz, a middle school math teacher in Oldham County, Kentucky, and Winn Wheeler, her instructional coach, created the anchor chart seen in Figure I.2 after students had read and analyzed various vignettes about famous people with different mindsets.

Figure I.2: Mindset Anchor Chart

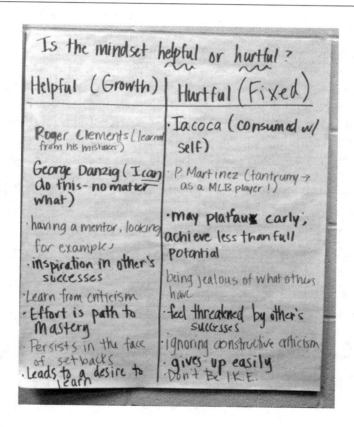

Finally, students need choices in their learning. You will visit teachers who use choice to allow students to access difficult reading. You will read how they plan backward to ensure students' access to *Othello* by focusing on the students' multiple intelligences. Their work prompted one of their students to conclude, "Limiting choice is like limiting the potential of the student; the more choice the student is offered, the greater their possibilities of succeeding." This is what access is all about.

What Will You Be Reading?

The Just-Right Challenge paints pictures of practice: classrooms where teachers have created the context for engaging students in doing important, relevant, challenging intellectual work. The teachers we have been fortunate to study, know the importance of attending to the academic work they offer students, know well how ready their students are for a challenge, and take the stance that all students can learn tough stuff if the teaching is done well. Most of the pictures of practice focus on urban students, but the principles underpinning the teaching practices are applicable to all students everywhere.

This book takes off from where our last one ended. In *Clock Watchers*, we argued that six components braided together best create the context for engagement: a caring classroom community, challenge, checking in/checking out (assessment), collaboration, choice, and celebration. All six of these Cs matter if a teacher is serious about creating a motivating classroom where the bottom line is deep learning. But we go further into challenge in this book, keeping Csikszentmihalyi's, Dweck's, and Moll's insights front and center. We show how the six Cs open the door for students to access the tough stuff of learning, and with the nine strategies that we explore in this book, teachers will be able to motivate and engage through the just-right challenge.

9 Strategies
1. Live the belief that students can "grow smartness"
2. Ferociously commit to students' potential
3. Maintain a passion for students as intellectuals
4. Make the work call for academic press
5. Provide work that is transformative
6. Ground the work in authenticity
7. Create a caring classroom community of learners
8. Check in to move forward
9. Build autonomy through choice

Each Part of the book opens and closes with a "Window into Practice" section, vignettes of very familiar practices that we see in classrooms across the country. The opening vignettes describe moments in the classroom before a teacher has reflected on stance, the nature of the work, or student access. We invite our readers to reflect on those vignettes with these questions in mind: *How do the practices highlighted in the snapshot limit or enhance challenge? What might be the impact on students like Connor, Justin, or Jerardo?* Then, closing each Part, we return to the "Window into Practice," but this time we provide a new picture of that same classroom that shows how the classroom changed after coaching and reflection. We invite readers to consider those changes and their impact on students. The vignette sections that begin and end the three Parts of the book include only narration and description without explanations so our readers can think about the implication and do the exposition.

The Just-Right Challenge takes us deeper into more classrooms so that readers will close this book with a clearer understanding of how challenge can work in a variety of contexts and know what steps they can take to implement challenge in their own classrooms. In Part 1, we look at teaching stance. Chapter 1 defines *stance* and describes three key strategies that support a stance that leads to engagement through a just-right challenge. Chapter 2 focuses on routines and rituals that arise from a teaching stance that entices students to engage in intellectually demanding work.

Part 2 explores the nature of the academic work. In Chapter 3, you'll sit in on a high school math class as you learn about three key strategies that support challenging academic work that matters and that grows students. In Chapter 4, you'll see how several teachers have implemented academic work and meet one teacher who invites students to think critically—about the literature they read and, therefore, about the world around them.

In Part 3, you'll see how three key strategies for student access impact teacher planning and how informative assessment practices help teachers determine the appropriate level of challenge. You'll read how the six Cs of motivation and engagement provide access for all learners. Chapter 5 takes you into several classrooms to watch teachers creating access, and in Chapter 6, you'll see a middle school math department that removed ability tracking in order to increase the level of access to all students.

We close the book with an invitation—a plea—for all teachers to create classrooms and classroom cultures for students like Connor, Justin, and Jerardo, classrooms where students want to linger because they are growing and are a part of the game of learning.

Through pictures of practice, we show the importance of having students do the work of thinking, reading, writing, and talking. As budding mathematicians, writers, historians, or scientists, they must be actively involved during the majority of class time. We nurture students' interest in being in the game by offering a route into deep understanding of the rules of the game and providing the time to put on those intellectual sweatpants and hustle out onto the court.

Our Teachers

Our book is filled with stories from the classroom, stories of teachers who have worked hard to grow their practice. None of the teachers would claim that they have "arrived," but all of them talk about their next steps as learners. You will meet teachers from urban high schools, mostly in the Denver area, and a few from the suburbs. Some of the teachers we write about teach in rural settings. We wanted to capture teachers' stories from a variety of contexts as we thought hard about the relationship between challenge and growth.

On to the Game of Learning

Imagine playing a game without clearly understanding the rules. You get more and more frustrated as the whistle signals mistakes you had no idea you were making. If the coach insists you continue playing without building your deep understanding of how to play the game, you will grow disillusioned and gradually begin to hate the game. Teachers can make a difference so that students not only remain in but succeed at the game of school.

Our book is a salute to those amazing teachers!

Teaching Stance

Window into Practice: Before

As you read this vignette, think about what Mrs. Green's actions suggest about her beliefs and assumptions about students. What do you notice about her stance toward students and learning? What's your hunch about how that stance shapes student learning? At the end of Part 1, you'll return to her classroom to see what changes occurred after her stance shifted.

As the twelve boys sauntered in the room, Mrs. Green, their special education teacher, welcomed each of them.

"Good to see you, Michael."

"Jonathan, I hope you got your homework done for math. Your math teacher stopped by to talk to me about your missing assignments." Jonathan nonchalantly nodded at her as he plopped into his desk. The desks, arranged in four neat rows, faced her desk. On the bulletin board was a list of the class rules and tips on how to read a short story. When the bell rang, she pointed to the assignment on the board and then read it to them. "Open your books to 'The Monkey's Paw' on page 62."

"I'm going to start reading, and then it'll be your turn." She started, "'Without, the night was cold and wet.'"

While she read, Michael looked down at his cell phone, which was tucked behind his opened book. Quickly he sent a text message. Mrs. Green's voice rattled him. "What's the main character called? What's the term for it? Michael, what do you think?"

He shrugged.

"You know it. We talked about it yesterday."

When he shrugged again, she gave him a hint. "It starts with a *p*. Pro . . . Come on, you know it."

Lionel hollered out, "Protagonist."

She smiled at him and nodded. "Who can tell me the name of the protagonist in this story?"

Silence.

"Jonathan, who do you think is the protagonist?"

He shook his head and looked away from her.

"Take a look at what I just read to you. Who do you think it might be?"

He continued looking away.

Lionel raised his hand and then blurted out, "The father."

"And what's the father's name?"

"Mr. White."

"Good," praised Mrs. Green. "And who is the father talking to?"

When no one answered, Mrs. Green called on Lionel, whose hand was again waving madly. The other boys were either slumped in their desks with heads on their arms or staring into space. "His son."

"Good. Who can tell me what time of day it is? In order to understand the story, it's important that you know this."

When no one answered, she told them that the story took place at night and then called on Brandon to read. Brandon glanced up from his hoodie and haltingly started to read.

The class continued with the students taking turns reading, Mrs. Green posing questions about the plot to make sure they understood, a few students reluctantly answering, and Lionel's hand waving away.

> If you're not making mistakes, then you're not doing anything. I'm positive that a doer makes mistakes. —**John Wooden**

CHAPTER 1

Classrooms to Linger In

Teachers in the Spotlight

Sherry Long is a middle school English teacher in Kentucky who teaches language arts and works with students who struggle as readers.

For years, **Lesli Cochran** was a middle school language arts and humanities teacher in Colorado. She currently teaches at an alternative school and works with students who have been unsuccessful in traditional schools.

Emily Skrobkro, a middle school science teacher in Denver, never intended to be a teacher, but once in the classroom, she has never regretted her decision to teach.

Negar Mizani is a high school English teacher in Denver. Negar witnessed the restructuring of one school with an extremely low performance rating, then moved on to another urban high school where she works with students in both regular and advanced tracks.

Teaching Stance

When we visit classes where teachers challenge students in a way that motivates and engages, we notice that there is a particular way in which they approach teaching. Even in vastly different contexts, there's a similarity in how teachers orchestrate unit plans, answer questions, decorate the room, and arrange the desks. We've catalogued concrete differences, such as the flow and tenor of conversation, and then listened to teachers talk about the beliefs that shape their practices. We've listened to students talk about those classrooms and identify what happened that made a difference for them. These are places where students want to linger, where we want our kids and grandkids to hang out and to learn.

What we see in these classrooms is a marriage of a certain set of beliefs to an almost predictable set of actions. We refer to this marriage as the *teaching stance*: the way a teacher stands in relationship to curriculum, instruction, and students. A teacher's stance is revealed in the language she uses, the classroom's routines and rituals, and the moment-by-moment instructional decisions. When you see it, you know it.

The importance of stance became clear a few years ago when coaching one of the kindest teachers we'd ever met: Sherry Long. Sherry is a teacher in Kentucky, the mother all of us wanted, someone who nurtured and loved unconditionally. Sherry welcomed students into her room, hovered near them in a protective manner whenever they needed comfort, and noticed when someone had on something new or had their hair brushed into a new style. Rarely did she utter an unkind or harsh word, even when the school's troublemaker sashayed into her room. When she talked about her teaching, she clearly explained her stance: she was there to protect her students. They had enough suffering in their lives, and she did not want them to have one more worry. Their lives were tough enough, and school didn't need to add to their struggles.

Ironically, this stance of protectiveness had negative consequences. Sherry avoided asking her most struggling students anything but easy questions. She selected literature to study that was easily accessible, and if anything was challenging, she would mitigate the challenge, sometimes by reading text to them and sometimes by giving them a worksheet that explained the intellectual moves they needed to make. Sherry's stance prevented her from doing what would move her students most: challenge them with tough stuff and then provide the scaffolding that would move them intellectually. By ensuring that students bypassed stress, Sherry limited their cognitive growth. But when she adjusted her stance, her students stepped up, became engaged, and embarked on a quality of work that awed her.

Conversation About the Common Core State Standards: Teacher Stance

Realizing the prominence of the Common Core State Standards, John and Stevi reflected on how their work connects with the era of new standards. What follows is an excerpt of their conversation:

John: Remember when we first started working on our book? The mantra we heard over and over was "rigor, relevance, and relationships." The last thing on our minds was a set of new standards, so it's interesting to realize that the

Common Core State Standards are attempting to take the nation's schools to the place that we were writing about.

Stevi: But what a difference in approach. We studied really smart teachers who were getting kids to do engaging and tough work. By watching them, we noticed and named the strategies they were using. Then Common Core came along and mandated what we noticed. While our work has been about inviting teachers to reflect on their stance and their practices, the Common Core is about imposing a way of thinking about school—and in many ways imposing the right thing. The approach is just so different.

John: It's one thing to ask students to do challenging work or, as the Common Core states, engage with rigorous content. But before we can get serious about the standards, we have to investigate what we believe about teaching and learning. We have to check in to see if we *really* believe that all students can do that kind of work. And as reflective practitioners, we have to do that frequently. Let me tell you what I did last week. I was planning the first night of the pedagogy course that I teach at the university. Since it's a follow-up to a course students had just completed, I wanted to review the key concepts of that first course. So I planned a lesson with some mundane and, frankly, boring activities. Then it hit me that I needed to challenge my students. I went from the boring, low-level review work to creating problems for them to solve using the content from the first course. What a reminder of how easy it is to fall back into the stance of just getting content covered.

Stevi: And we know that pressure to cover content is tremendous. Right now what I'm nervous about are some of the critiques of Common Core—and, believe me, I have my own critique. But too many of the critiques express doubts that students can do complex work even with smart instructional support.

John: Nothing in Common Core asks educators to investigate what they believe about kids and whether they believe that students are able to do tough work. What we've learned is, that's the key.

Stevi: Yes, teacher stance matters!

High Expectations and Stance

Stance can differ even when teachers voice similar beliefs. Take a look at Marshall's and Lesli's classes. Even though Lesli taught at a middle school and Marshall at high school, they talked about their beliefs in a similar way. Both believed in holding expectations high and that with effort all students can do intellectually tough work. But when we heard students talk about the two teachers, we knew something was different. Lesli's class seemed to be a place we wanted to linger in, but Marshall's sure wasn't. A look into their classrooms reveals that while beliefs might be similar, manifestations of those beliefs can be vastly different.

On Marshall's classroom wall was a sign straight from Dante: "Abandon hope all ye who enter here." Marshall welcomed new students by stressing how tough he was and made sure they knew he wouldn't accept anything less than excellence from them. "If you can't meet my expectations, you know where the counselors are," he told students. This was his stance: he'll hold expectations high, and it's up to the students, not him, to make sure they meet them.

On the other hand, Lesli explained, "One of the things I believe is that not all kids are going to love reading, and that's fine. What's not fine is kids' not being able to figure out tough text. That's what I'm going to make sure they can do." She held those expectations high and then provided the strategies, modeling, and practice that students needed to reach those expectations. Her stance was clear: I expect you to be smart, and together we'll make sure you get there.

A look at how the two teachers arranged their room provided further hints about their different stances. Marshall's room was arranged in six rows of five desks, all neatly lined up and facing his desk. On his walls were professionally made posters with quotes from Shakespeare, Thoreau, and Vonnegut. Marshall's desk commanded the spotlight, and the posters reflected authors he loved. In Lesli's room the chairs were arranged in a semicircle, three rows deep. Her desk was nestled in the corner of the room. When students sat, they faced each other, not Lesli. On one bulletin board were samples of student writing and articles from the local newspaper that her students had written. The unit's essential question was on one board, and on another was an anchor chart that listed different ways that questions help kids to understand difficult text. Instead of Lesli's passions being front and center, she spotlighted student work. Just looking at the rooms, one could infer that Marshall's stance was more teacher-centered and Lesli's student-centered.

Actions are based on reason; it's the rare behavior that is displayed "just because." Something sits behind all the moves we make: an assumption, examined or unexamined; a belief, realistic or unrealistic; or perhaps a tradition, still appropriate or long past its usefulness. We've learned that teachers who seem to create magic in their classrooms share certain beliefs and assumptions that prop up their teaching stance. We've formulated these beliefs and assumptions into three strategies: live the belief that students can "grow smartness," ferociously commit to students' potential, and maintain an unwavering passion for students as intellectuals. Through watching the language these teachers use as they talk with their students, looking at the setup of their rooms, and noticing the different kinds of instructional activities they design, we've seen how these strategies are manifested in their stance. The result is the kind of learning we would want for all students.

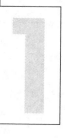

Strategy 1: Live the Belief That Students Can "Grow Smartness"

What Sherry, our nurturing, kind teacher, came to understand later in her teaching career is what Carol Dweck (2006) refers to as a "growth mindset." This is the mindset, or way of thinking, that we find in all teachers who are successful at challenging students. Even if those teachers have never heard of Carol Dweck's work, the belief that students can grow their smartness buoys their actions.

Early in her professional work, Dweck watched two groups of children struggle with some difficult puzzles. As the puzzles grew in complexity, the researchers expected students to become frustrated and give up when they could no longer solve them. One group did exactly as predicted, but not so another group. Several of the students in the second group talked about the fun they were having with the increased challenge: "Not only were they not discouraged by failing, they didn't know they were failing. They thought they were learning" (2006, 4). This group of children exhibited what Dweck came to call a "growth mindset" because they believed that eventually with effort they could figure out challenging problems. In contrast, Dweck called the mindset of the first group "fixed." For them, their intelligence is unmalleable. Talents, personality, and intellectual capacity are predetermined, and what one is born with is what one is either stuck with or blessed with. One of the consequences of this fixed mindset is that people work at protecting and validating their self-image, avoiding situations that threaten their view of themselves. So instead of developing their skills and intellectual capacities, they work at confirming and validating their beliefs.

Long before Stevi was familiar with Dweck's work, she saw the fixed mindset in action as she worked with adolescent readers. She watched as some struggling readers became entrapped in a cycle of failure. Whenever they had difficulties comprehending, they felt frustrated and began to avoid reading in general. Avoidance leads to lack of practice, which results in no improvement. Along the way such learners' sense of confidence in their ability to read and, consequently, the motivation to pick up a book continues to wane. Stanovich (1986) calls this the "Matthew Effect"—the successful reader gets better and better because of practice while the less skilled reader's failure at reading increases because of lack of practice. Time and time again Stevi saw the impact of this cycle of failure with her middle and high school students (see Figure 1.1).

Although Stevi early on recognized the results of a fixed mindset among some students, what she didn't realize at the time is that the same cycle impacts gifted and talented students. As a young girl, Carol Dweck remembers well: "If you could arrange successes and avoid failures (at all costs), you could stay smart" (2006, 4). When a student with a fixed mindset has a choice of doing something at the edges of his limit, he tends to avoid it; he plays it safe.

Figure 1.1: Cycle of Failure

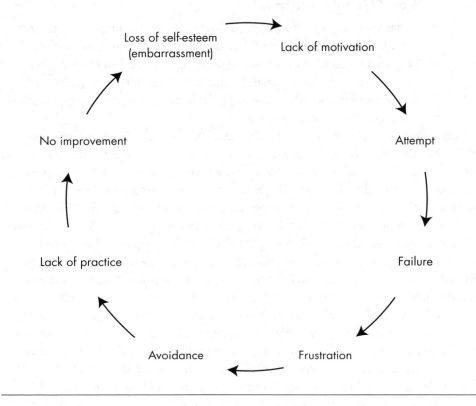

Sadly, the fixed mindset has dominated educators' minds as well for some time. Walk into any teacher's lounge and you'll hear it:

- "It's my special ed kids. You know they can't do well on that test."
- "Watch my gifted and talented kids. They are amazing."
- "What do you expect? Look at where he comes from."
- "IB is too tough for him. He'll never make it."

Students too often talk about themselves from a fixed mindset:

- "I never was any good at math."
- "English is easy. I'm a pretty good writer."
- "I just don't have any talent drawing."

Imagine, though, a teacher (and student) who views students through a growth mindset. Here are some typical comments we've heard from teachers successful at challenging students (and we do mean students from different kinds of backgrounds, even some very tough backgrounds):

- "Yes, they're far behind, so we have a lot of work to do."
- "Of course, you haven't done well on the state assessment. Look at how many times you've moved and how you're still learning to speak English. But this year, we're going to get you caught up."
- "It's a struggling group of kids, but we're going to change that."
- "Yes, they lack skills right now, but they still deserve to learn to access the challenging material with my help."

Growth Mindset in Action

Lesli Cochran, the middle school teacher who stressed the importance of students' being able to navigate tough text, would not have credited Dweck for informing her stance. However, as we watched Lesli interact with students, we saw Dweck's theory in action and how that theory shaped her teaching.

Lesli was clear about her stance: students needed to do hard work, and, therefore, her role was to find a way into the learning, design the necessary scaffolds, and provide the space for students to succeed. Lesli knew that many of her students were convinced of their lack of ability and had little hope that their efforts would pay off. Caitlyn, one of her eighth graders, stated, "I wasn't a very good reader, and most of my teachers didn't think that I could read." In prior years, if she read three books a year—often only those assigned to her—that was quite the accomplishment. By the end of eighth grade, however, Caitlyn had read over forty books, impressing herself, her parents, and her peers. She had learned that she could grow as a reader. Lesli understood that some of her students, such as Caitlyn, didn't know *how* to exert the effort, so she showed them how to develop the kind of intellectual effort that produced results. She built a sense of competency and agency.

A peek into her classroom illustrates the growth mindset in action. As you read, pay particular attention to the language Lesli used and notice how that language reinforced student effort. You'll see how she celebrated students' accomplishments, welcomed their confusions, and then led the way for them to untangle their understanding. By listening in on Lesli talking with her students, we get a picture of how this stance nudges students' progress.

Mostly Hispanic and mostly from families of poverty, this class of eighth graders did not reflect the academic diversity of the school. Every student in Lesli's class had a label and some, multiple labels: self-selective-mute, autistic, troublemaker, probationer, English language learner, learning disabled. A few of the students had parents they visited in prison, and a couple didn't know where their mom and dad were—their foster parents were the only family that they knew. Many students had an Individualized Education Plan (IEP) and an Individual Literacy Plan (ILP) that traveled with them. One student had attended eleven schools in the past eight years while several others had been together since kindergarten. But someone who didn't know their backgrounds wouldn't have realized this by watching the classroom that day because their teacher looked beyond labels to recognize strengths and envision possibilities.

For the first fifteen to twenty minutes of each class, Lesli's students read books of their choice while she conferred with them. Her first conference of the day was with Jerardo. (Remember him from the introduction?) Kneeling down by him, she asked, "How's it going?"

"I'm almost done."

"That's why I wanted to talk to you today. Just think: you've finished two books already even this early in the year." She high-fived him. He laughed and then quietly told her that he's getting a little confused. Lesli asked, "So if it's confusing, how are you keeping track?"

Her question suggested that he needed to track his ideas and come from the positive presupposition that he would and that he knew how. Confusion isn't something to avoid or to fear, but it presents an opportunity to stretch. Lesli trusted that her students would be reading books just slightly beyond their range, so she knew that the way to keep them reading was to give them tools and the encouragement to keep on going.

Jerardo explained what he was doing about his confusion, "I'm trying to figure out what's important and what I need to pay attention to." Because Lesli has taught the students cognitive strategies for comprehending text (Tovani 2000, 2004), she expected them to use the language of thinking, but she wanted to make sure Jerardo could apply those strategies.

"What do you mean by determining importance? What does that look like?" After listening to him, she knew she needed to coach him by naming what he was doing and then by slowing him down a bit. "You're using multiple strategies at once. Awesome. Let's start with inferring first. How does that work with you?" He explained and she validated his thinking and then reframed it. "That's such a smart thing to do, but I'm thinking that you're doing something a little bit more sophisticated. So you've told me you used background knowledge to make an inference, but then you asked a question and at that point reread. The second time around you changed your strategy, and finally it made sense. When I get confused and reread, I have to change strategies or else I'll just stay stuck. That was a good move you made. I want you to watch how you finish the book, and let me know if you're satisfied with the ending. Don't forget to bring a new book tomorrow."

Lesli just prompted Jerardo into doing more cognitively sophisticated work. By naming what he was doing in his head, she nurtured a growth mindset so that Jerardo would be clear that he had the ability and the skills to make sense of difficult text. At the start of the year, Jerardo, like many of his classmates, had been convinced that he didn't have the intellectual gift to read well and to figure out what to do when he became confused. The belief that his intelligence was fixed could easily have trailed him throughout his life unless someone showed him what to do when confused and then gently nudged him to practice that kind of thinking. Had Lesli simply praised him, her instruction wouldn't have had the same power to move him. By naming what he did and by focusing on what next steps he could take, she showed him that he could and would continue to get smarter. Lesli's language reflected her stance: with support, time, and practice, all students would learn and grow.

Even the way that Lesli praised Jerardo was supportive of a growth mindset. According to Dweck's research, praise that is global, such as "you're such a talented artist," reinforces a fixed mindset while praise that focuses on effort reflects the growth mindset (see Figure 1.2). In some studies students who were given praise that focused on their effort increased their performance substantially. According to one study of four hundred fifth graders by Dweck and her team at Columbia University quoted by Robin Moroney in his blog (2007):

> [T]he children took three tests. The second test purposely was made difficult enough that every child failed. What the scientists found was that kids who had been praised for their *effort* recovered from that failure by the third test to achieve scores 30% higher than on their first test. Meanwhile, the students who were praised for their *intelligence* had scores that were 20% lower. Ms. Dweck's conclusion: You should praise children for qualities they can control, like effort. Those praised for their innate brainpower might develop the sense that hard work isn't necessary.

Lesli's praise of Jerardo focused on effort time and time again:

- "You're using multiple strategies at once. Awesome."
- "Just think: you've finished two books already." She high-fived him.

Figure 1.2: Comment-Belief-Impact Chart

Teacher comment	Inferred belief	Impact on student
How's it going?	The student is doing serious, important work and can be metacognitive.	Builds efficacy.
If it's confusing, how are you keeping track?	Confusion isn't a bad thing; there's something that you can do.	Trusts the student as problem solver.
Let's figure out what you can do when you get stuck, especially since you don't have much background knowledge yet.	A student can power though difficulties if the student has strategies.	Builds a set of strategies to do tough stuff.

Strategy 2: Ferociously Commit to Students' Potential

Emily Skrobko is another teacher whose classroom we love to linger in. A middle school science teacher in Denver, Emily loves her work and tears up when she talks about teaching. Teaching had not been in her career plans, but when she graduated with a biology degree, she wasn't sure what to do. As a lark, she accepted a job teaching with an emergency license and then returned to school to earn her teaching credentials. While student teaching, she watched her mentor teacher in awe. "It was as if she were sprinkling magic fairy dust over the class. And I wanted to be able to do that." And as we sat in her classes where challenge motivated and engaged, it indeed seemed like her class, too, was sprinkled with that fairy dust.

Her year had not started this way, however. "I had two distinct groups of kids. My morning students were regular kids who were curious about science, but the afternoon class was filled with students with special needs and students who resisted learning science. On their preassessment, the afternoon students' scores were half those of the morning students. For the first quarter of the year, she confessed that she was frustrated and struggled. Later in the year, we checked in to see what was happening in Emily's afternoon class. "It's like night and day," Emily explained. "They're working hard and growing."

"What changed?" Stevi probed.

"Me. I realized that I had to adjust my attitude, and it made a world of difference."

Emily explained that after quite a bit of reflection, she realized that she had lowered her expectations for her afternoon students and that this needed to change. "When I became clear that they could do the same work as my morning class, things began to shift. I realized that they might need more scaffolding, but they could do it—and it has paid off. Sure, it takes more time for my afternoon class to understand big concepts, but they're getting there." She explained that students were more respectful with each other and more engaged. "I had let some of the kids pull out of discussions, something that I never do with my morning class, so I stopped doing that with them. Instead I insisted that all of them participate and didn't give them a choice." Her commitment, belief in the students, and raised expectations made a huge difference. On the midyear interim assessments, she saw an equal amount of growth in the two classes. Sure, the morning scores were higher, but the students in the afternoon class were growing, and they knew it.

A few days after this conversation, we talked to students in classrooms we had studied. Negar Mizani, a high school teacher in Denver, taught English. As we listened to her students, we realized how essential this commitment to student potential is, no matter what the circumstances. Even though the high school where Negar taught was in the process of being closed because of the unpleasant distinction of having the state's lowest test scores, she saw each student's potential and refused to lower her expectations. Her students recognized how her passion for her curriculum, coupled with her passion for her students, drove them to work hard and succeed. From these conversations, another belief emerged that informed the stances of these remarkable teachers: a ferocious commitment to student potential. The students most elegantly described how these teachers manifested this commitment: through personal and collective regard.

Personal Regard

In *Clock Watchers* (2009) we posited that a caring classroom community was a prerequisite for a motivating and engaging classroom, and in our current research, we saw again how important this is. A classroom community is created purposefully and intentionally, and students recognize this. (See Chapter 2 for more about developing routines and rituals that create a strong sense of classroom community.)

The first sign of the caring classroom community was that teachers made sure they knew their students and regularly interacted with them on a personal level, not as friends but as mentors. Negar's student Jacqueline explained: "She asked me how my day was going and asked about my family. She was one of the only teachers who did that and one of the few teachers who got to know us. She doesn't look down at you, but looks up at you." At the height of her teenage cynicism, Jacqueline contrasted Negar with teachers who had what she called an "I'm-the-teacher" attitude and who showed up just to collect a paycheck. Negar, on the other hand, "was a mentor, committed to you and insistent on growth." Similarly, Lesli Cochran's students described her as a parent who knew them well enough to push them hard.

High expectations follow on the heels of personal regard. As we discussed in *Clock Watchers*, these teachers were "warm demanders" (Gay 2000), insisting that students care about their intellectual work and about the quality of that work. This is the payoff for this stance. One of Lesli's students explained, "We can choose to work or not to work, but if we don't do our work she will hunt us down."

And the connection to challenge? To getting in the academic game? Over and over, we heard students tell us that because their teacher cared, they worked harder. Jacqueline explained, "I can't let her down. I used to be a bare minimum student because I never had a teacher I could relate to. I didn't feel like I was smart, but she showed me that I am."

"I could not come to her class unprepared," June explained. "If I did, I felt like I let her down. She believed in my ability to succeed, therefore, I believed in myself."

One of Lesli's middle school students stated, "She pushes us more than other teacher because she knows our potential."

And they rose to that challenge.

Funds of Knowledge

Closely connected to personal regard is the concept of funds of knowledge (Moll et al. 2001). Many teachers who work with urban students are acutely aware of what students do not bring into the classroom and, sadly, some complain about students' lack of "cultural capital," perceiving students through the lens of deficits. Lesli, Negar, Emily, and the other teachers we've studied, however, were driven by a very different belief, which shaped their classroom stance. Mirroring Moll et al.'s theory of funds of knowledge, they recognized the assets that students brought into the classroom. The concept of funds of knowledge is based on an important but relatively simple premise: *all* students, including students of poverty, students new to English, and students whose parents have a grade-school education, are filled with knowledge derived from their life experiences. Students are not blank slates nor are their heads empty vessels waiting to be filled; instead, they bring to the classroom a lifetime of experiences and community resources, called their funds of knowledge. More formally, researchers define funds of knowledge as "the historically accumulated and culturally developed bodies of knowledge and skills essential for household or individual functioning and well-being" (Moll et al. 2001, 133).

A teacher with such a stance doesn't look at students who walk into her room from the deficit model; instead, a teacher sees that students bring with them a pool of knowledge, perhaps different from what the school typically values, but nonetheless valuable to them in their world. This doesn't mean that the teacher blithely ignores students' misconceptions, partial understandings, or gaps in knowledge. Instead, she recognizes them but recognizes and values their strengths as well, then builds from those assets.

Again, the teachers we studied typified this belief, which underpinned their stances. They knew that by working from students' strengths and staying attuned to students' funds of knowledge, students could perform. Gonzales, Moll, and Amanti (2005) also found this to be true when they studied a group of Spanish-speaking students in a remedial reading program. They suspected that students could do more challenging work than what was being asked of them. Those suspicions were confirmed when they shifted instruction to match students' funds of knowledge and academic performance improved.

Emily Skrobko's classroom brings this concept to life. Daily, she talked to students about their background knowledge and the importance of tapping into that knowledge as they thought about scientific conundrums. "Kids' background knowledge is powerful, and it's my job to figure out what they bring to class." When she conferred with students, she regularly asked them what they already knew about the content under study. She asked them to think about what the problem reminded them of and what they already knew about similar topics. She used analogies grounded in their world to help them connect to the new content under study. By posing questions and by insisting that they think about their daily lives, she showed them that they can figure out academic problems.

Collective Regard

Along with valuing individual students and honoring the funds of knowledge they bring to the class, these teachers also attend carefully to the community of the classroom as a whole, and students recognize this. A year after she had left Negar's class, Jacqueline remembered clearly the mantra, "Listen with your ears, eyes, and heart."

Lesli's students talked about how at the start of the year they were worried about who they'd be with in class: "We had so many different types of people in class. We wondered if we would get along and who was going to be whose partner. Now we can be partners with anyone." The students were clear that they could never make fun of each other because "Ms. Cochran would get angry."

Because these classrooms are emotionally and psychologically safe, students were able to take intellectual risks that they may not have taken in other contexts. For example, toward the end of the school year, students in Lesli's class had to write and prepare a speech—not an unusual task for a language arts class, but for eighth graders, this can be a terrifying experience. Nevertheless, these students had the confidence that they could talk about topics that really mattered to them because of the classroom community. Alan, an autistic student who was new to the school, had never talked in detail about life with autism. Because the class was safe, he delivered one of the most important speeches of his young life. He knew that for the first time in his nine years in school, he had thirty friends who would listen and support him. As one of his peers said, "No one would pick on each other. We stand up for each other." And he knew "that Ms. Cochran would stop anyone who made a rude comment."

One of the results of creating this kind of a community is that students move beyond compliance and into engagement. Students often talked about how in some classes they did the work but had no investment in learning the content. However, in a class where a teacher and other classmates care, they became serious about the work they were doing. The work took on meaning and purpose in a way that didn't happen in other contexts.

We witnessed another interaction that shows what can happen when a classroom community is strong. Vincent and Thomas, students in Emily's eighth-grade science class, were working as partners during a pair/share discussion. Thomas understood the concept under study, but Vincent wasn't as clear. When Thomas asked Vincent about his thoughts on the question Emily had posed, Vincent shrugged, "I have no idea." Thomas, however, kept asking questions, prompting Vincent to think about the question. Finally, Vincent got the concept and Thomas smiled, complimenting him on how he figured it out. Thomas became the teacher, showing through his questions and his body language that he cared about whether Vincent understood.

What more could a teacher ask for?

Strategy 3: Maintain a Passion for Students as Intellectuals

Back in the '90s, the high school where John and Stevi taught was toying around with joining the Coalition of Essential Schools. They witnessed and participated in debates around the Common Principles that under-pinned CES schools. One principle in particular fueled heated conver-sation: "Student as worker, teacher as coach: **The governing practical metaphor of the school should be student-as-worker, rather than the more fa-miliar metaphor of teacher-as-deliverer-of-instructional-services. Accordingly, a prominent pedagogy will be coaching, to provoke students to learn how to learn and thus to teach themselves**" (www.essentialschools.org/items/4). Some teachers argued that the teacher's job was to provide the content before the students could be the workers and doubted that abandoning the teacher-as-deliverer-of-instructional-services would serve students well.

However, in the classrooms where we watched teachers sprinkle that magic fairy dust that Emily talked about, we've seen over and over the wisdom of this principle. In fact, the belief that students can be and *must* be the intellectual workers in the classroom powerfully influences their teaching stance.

Listen to Emily: "I want them to know they can do the thinking. I'm not a crutch." She sees her job as showing students how to do the thinking but not doing it for them. And how does this belief inform her actions? She explained, "When students don't answer when I ask their thoughts on something, I wait and then I wait some more. My expectation is that you have to think and you have to answer." But she also understands the role of scaffolding. When she "cold-calls" on students, she provides them the chance to think/share first. "Anytime I do 'cold calling,' I do pair/share first. This is why you talk to a partner—you can use their thinking. I just don't accept not thinking."

Here's what Lesli Cochran had to say about the goals for her students:

> One of my goals . . . is to provide the opportunity for intellectual discourse. I really want them to be able to sit with one another and talk about big ideas in the world. I want them to challenge one another—and me when it comes to ideas that matter. This is the root of my work this year.

To illustrate how this belief translates into a teaching stance, read how Lesli led students in a discussion. Since her stance was informed by her belief that students must be the intellectual workers in the classroom, she urged them to engage in difficult thinking and to challenge each other throughout the discussion.

The Boy in the Striped Pajamas

Midway into a study of the Holocaust, the students were reading *The Boy in the Striped Pajamas*. Lesli knew that student readiness was important to their eventual success in understanding the novel and growing as thinkers. Early on the book had been challenging, but Lesli slowly built students' background knowledge by bringing in short texts about the Holocaust. Some of the texts were newspaper clippings from the '30s and '40s while others were primary documents from that era. Lesli's plan was to deepen their understanding about the Holocaust and teach them how they could be strategic in solving problems they might encounter as they read difficult text in the future. Time and time again she gauged their readiness to go deeper and reflected on how much more scaffolding they needed or what scaffolding she needed to remove. Providing students access to difficult content was front and center in her mind as she planned and as she taught.

"Yesterday we looked at how inferences assist us in understanding difficult text. Today we're going to look at questions and how they can help us when we get bored or when we get stuck. Let's generate questions from that text you're holding in your hands and then see if we can figure out how to answer to them. We'll think also about how those questions would keep us reading."

"How did Hitler come to power?" asked Robert. Lesli put that on the document camera.

Annie asked, "I have a question. Why did Hitler pick on the Jews?"

After several more questions had been generated, Lesli paused them. "Let's think about those questions. To figure out how to answer them, I might go to the Internet, or I might visit the library and pick a book like this one." She held up *Hitler Youth*. "Will this book help me answer Annie's question or Robert's?" When no one answered, she continued. "What do you think this book will be about? What would you do to find out?"

Annie says, "Skim and scan."

"What else?" As usual, Lesli refused to settle on one idea. She pushed her students to generate more possibilities.

"Who says the answer's not in here? Come on, Jerardo. Fight with me."

Jerardo asserted, "I think we should try a different book."

Jorge interrupted, "But what if his dad hated the Jews? Then *Hitler Youth* might give us an answer."

Lesli asked, "So do you think that prejudice comes from families? That's another question that we might ask ourselves to move us along. Where else do we get our prejudice?" The class explored these questions for a while, and Lesli jotted down their questions precisely as they posed them. By using their exact words, she buffered their thinking, honoring their curiosity and valuing their language.

Convinced that her students had to be the intellectual workers in the classroom, she continued to push, nudge, and scaffold their learning. Her passion for their ability to think meant that her stance was one of listening, asking, and insisting on their figuring out the problems they encountered.

This strategy also can serve as a foundation for the adult learner. Wendy Hoffer-Ward, a math and science consultant and author of several books, is the master of this strategy when she works with adults. "I love to give them difficult math problems and model the thinking needed to solve the problem. Then I move them into groups and trust that they'll figure out it." Wendy refuses to answer any question that the group can figure out. "If I answer it, what is that saying about who they are as intellectuals? It's distrusting them and undercutting what they're capable of."

Wendy's and Lesli's position reflects Peter Johnston's insights:

> . . . there are hidden costs in telling people things. If a student can figure something out for him- or herself, explicitly providing the information preempts the student's opportunity to build a sense of agency and independence, which, in turn, affects the relationship between teacher and student. Think about it. When you figure out something for yourself, there is a thrill in the figuring. (2004, 8)

That thrill in figuring out tough things works for all learners, regardless of their age.

Shifting Teacher Beliefs

The more we watched teachers and listened to students, the more certain we were that for all students to do difficult, challenging work, a teacher must reflect on and, if need be, adjust her stance so that it mirrors her beliefs and is, therefore, reflected in her practices.

Remember Sherry Long, the very caring teacher from Kentucky we met at the start of the chapter? Toward the end of the year, she had stopped rescuing her students, and, as a result, her classroom looked quite different. More students talked during whole-group discussions, and when they worked with partners, often the conversation was animated and energetic. The tenor of her room had changed. What happened? Sherry reflected on her stance about protecting her students and began responding differently to them. One of her favorite questions became: "And what do you think about that?" rather than answering their question. By shifting her practice, she shifted her stance. And the results? Students were much more engaged than they had been in the past.

How did she get there? Sherry was a highly reflective practitioner who was committed to getting better and better as a teacher. Despite a long career in teaching, she didn't rest on past practices and repeat lessons that had worked earlier. Instead, she read, welcomed a coach who nudged her to reflect, and learned ways to support students to become independent learners. Through practice, ongoing learning, and opening her classroom for feedback, she grew. And so did her kids.

Eventually her teaching stance became an unwavering commitment to students to do challenging work, and therefore it was her job to find intriguing text, pose magnetic questions, and model ways of doing the smart work that students were capable of doing.

For Emily to make shifts in her practices, she first needed a vision to see what was possible. Emily was visibly moved as she described visiting a fourth-grade classroom with students from a neighborhood similar to the one her students came from. "Those kids were thinking better than my middle school students were. I wanted that for my students." So she set out to learn how to get her students to do that kind of thinking and continued to reflect on her teaching stance, carefully assessing whether her practices matched her evolving beliefs. When she noticed that she was answering her students' questions too quickly, she realized she wasn't letting them be the intellectual thinkers she believed they could be, so she began to shift how she responded. When she saw that they wasted too much time getting ready to work at the start of class, she reflected on her opening routines, noticed that they didn't reflect her beliefs in building background knowledge, and shifted her practices. And who gains from this shift in stance? Those human beings who fill our classrooms and deserve to be challenged.

Reflection

YOUR LANGUAGE

Record fifteen minutes of your classroom and then complete this chart:

Reflection on Language		
What did you say? (Teacher comment)	What's the belief that sits under the comment?	What might be the impact on students?

By recording your language, you can begin to surface your stance for reflection. What language do you need to shift so that it mirrors your beliefs?

YOUR ACTIONS

Now take stock of a typical class. What do you do? What do students do? What would an observer infer about your stance toward learning, curriculum, thinking, and challenge? Complete the following table and see what you learn about your practices.

Reflection on Actions			
Action	Reason or belief about teaching and learning that guides this action	What is the impact on student learning of this action?	What would an observer infer about your stance?

YOUR ROOM

Look around your room. How are desks arranged? What's on your walls? What does this suggest about your stance?

> Children, in their own ways, teach us about the language of our classrooms.
>
> —**Peter Johnston,** *Choice Words*

CHAPTER 2

Teaching Stance Daily

Teachers in the Spotlight

 Lesli Cochran taught middle school humanities in a small town in Colorado for quite a few years before she moved to an alternative school where she now works with students ranging from their preteens to adulthood.

 Emily Skrobkro is a middle school science teacher in an urban school in Colorado.

 Alisa Wills-Keely teaches high school English and coaches other teachers in her building.

It was the start of the second day of our workshop in a small township outside of Dundee, South Africa. Karen, Sheila, and Stevi were reviewing the upcoming day's plan when Sbo marched into the drab classroom. Since Sbo, who grew up here, had initially contacted Karen about working with her teachers on writing pedagogy, they suspected that she was early for official business.

"Follow me," she commanded.

Sbo led them to the community room, and there, standing in a large circle, were the teachers from the workshop. As they joined the circle, one voice—they couldn't tell whose—softly began a song, and soon other voices blended in as the teachers swayed to the music. Fiona drifted into the center of the circle and began dancing. Mbali joined her. Slowly the song faded, but before the last note was over, someone else started a new song, and the circle moved with this faster rhythm. Another teacher glided into the center to dance and then another and another.

And from that day on, they began the workshop this way: everyone circling up to sing, swaying to the rhythm of the music, and joining dance with song in the center of the circle. After about ten minutes, the singing faded, and they moved to the classrooms for the day's learning to begin. It was a poignant routine and ritual that set the stage for the teachers to learn and grow in community.

Working in South Africa for those couple of weeks taught Stevi many lessons, and the joy that came from this community routine and ritual was one of the gentlest and most moving lessons of all. It reminded her that in life outside of school we have our predictable routines and rituals that get us up and keep us going—true, routines not necessarily as poetic as the singing and dancing in Dundee, but still, routines and rituals that mark events and guide our thinking. When Stevi rises in the morning, she turns on the coffee pot, brushes her teeth, and hops into the shower. Before she writes, she grabs a cup of coffee, makes sure that her kitchen counter is clean, and utters the phrase, "butt in chair, butt in chair." Before her husband heads up to their small mountain cabin, she can predict that he will fill the plastic water jug, look at the crumpled list in his pocket to see what else he needs to bring, and double-check the counter in the garage for any items he means to take. These practices, as simple as they are, are the undercurrents of a well-run life, so automatic, so predictable that they become nearly invisible.

In many of the classrooms where we've seen students engaged in challenging work, routines and rituals were the rebar of instruction, supporting students as they did tough intellectual work. Students counted on those daily—or almost daily—practices, which became expected and resonated with significance. In Lesli Cochran's room, students were sure of reading at the start of each class, knowing she might pull up a chair next to them to have a conversation about their reading. In Emily Skrobko's middle school science class, students knew that class begins with reflecting on the day's learning targets and sharpening their observation skills by studying a Far Side cartoon. In Alisa Wills-Keely's high school English classroom, students knew that the topical question of the day would drive their work and that they might follow a discussion protocol as they worked collaboratively.

Routines and Rituals That Reflect Teaching Stance

For routines and rituals to create the kind of culture that builds intellectual muscle, they need to grow out of positive presuppositions about students. We're talking about the kinds of routines and rituals that build community and that nurture a culture of thinking where teamwork matters, where the intellectual work pertains to the student, and where the teacher maintains high expectations with support.

When we first started talking to teachers about routines and rituals, they spoke of connections to classroom management, but we meant something different. Classroom management is about establishing and maintaining control and squelching unruly behavior. It's the goal of the mantra from our early days of teaching: Don't smile until after Christmas. After all, we were told by veteran teachers, we had to make sure that students knew we meant serious business. No monkey business in this classroom! So we were advised to set up the rules that clarified the consequences for tardies, explained the need for raising hands before speaking, and listed the penalties for late work. And always, we were to set those rules with a straight face, nary a grin.

Establishing procedures through the lens of classroom management grew from a stance grounded in power, control, and consequences. Our thinking began with the negative: behavior we did not want to happen. It was, as Tomlinson and Imbeau (2011) said, teaching defensively. Our stance was supported by the belief that adolescents will misbehave unless we exert our authority and maintain distance. We set the rules, and their job was to follow them.

Remember Marshall? Marshall was a master at classroom management. The sign on his classroom wall reflected just that: "Abandon hope all ye who enter here." On the first few days of school he went over the classroom rules. "I used to have students develop the rules, but I decided that was a waste of time. The rules were about the same as what I wanted, so to save time I skip that step. They know I mean business; it's the rare kid who goofs off in my classroom."

Please don't misread what we are saying. Classroom management is important. After all, we all know that the downfall of most beginning teachers is a lack of classroom management. But when we're talking about routines and rituals, we're talking about managing a classroom through a very different stance. We're talking about design principles that provide the structure for students to do smart work and that begin with a passionate belief in students as intellectuals. We're talking about routines and rituals illuminated by the strategies we discussed in Chapter 1.

Stance matters.

Match Beliefs with Routines and Rituals

When Lesli first started teaching, she understood the power of good classroom management and set about developing rules for her classroom. Like Nuthall (2005), she knew the "ritualized routines" that led to compliant behavior. As Nuthall's research found, anyone who has spent ten years in school as a student understands that raising your hand is important, that teachers stand in front of the class, and that students listen diligently—or at least pretend to listen. There are routines that are ritualized simply out of ongoing practice year after year, generation after generation. This is not what we're talking about.

Many of Lesli's routines and rituals from those early days provided the structure students needed to be compliant and were ones that she had learned from her student teaching days or picked up at one workshop or another. But as she grew as a teacher, she needed to rethink those practices in order to be consistent with her new beliefs. At her instructional coach's urging, she made a chart with four columns. In the first column, she listed all her teaching moves, including those daily routines and rituals. Next to them, she jotted down the reason for using the particular practice. In the next column, she matched the practice and the reason with a teaching belief, and in the fourth column decided whether to keep, revise, or reject the practice (see Figure 2.1).

What she learned from this was that she still had some practices that had outlived her current beliefs. Convinced that her practices had to mirror her teaching stance, Lesli made some changes. As a result, no longer did she start class with a provocative quote that had nothing to do with what students were doing during the rest of the class, and no longer at the end of the hour did she ask brain teasers and reward students who knew the most answers. Those practices no longer fit.

Lesli's stance was solid: students could think hard about important ideas if given the support. What she wanted were routines and rituals that grew confident thinkers. She wanted every move in her classroom to be about ensuring that students were becoming more capable of independently tackling challenging work. Clear about the kind of intellectual challenge she wanted her students to engage in, Lesli figured out predictable routines to meet that goal.

Figure 2.1: Reflection on Routines and Rituals and Beliefs

Use this chart to reflect on your regular routines and rituals. In column one, list all those regular practices that you do day in and day out. Then name your reason for using it and the belief that sits behind the practice. Does that belief reflect the stance that you want to take? If it does, you'll want to keep it. If not, then perhaps it's time to revise or reject that practice.

Reflection on Routines and Rituals and Beliefs			
Routine/Ritual	Reason for it	Belief	Keep, revise or reject?

Different Kinds of Rituals and Routines

Routines and rituals serve myriad purposes. Some are regular practices that set the stage for learning, while others are practices that keep students on the stage and under the spotlight so that they are the key actors, the principle thinkers.

Setting the Stage

Not too long ago, Stevi toured Universal Studios in Los Angeles. While driving through the set of one of Stephen Spielberg's movies, the tour guide explained that the set director's job was to design sets that matched Mr. Spielberg's vision for the movie. Similarly, at the start of the school year, a teacher must be able to articulate her own vision and stance for her classroom by designing routines and rituals that will lead students to meet that vision and that are in synch with her stance. Once clear about her vision and stance, her design could begin by reflecting on several questions:

- What does the start of the year look like so that community is created and students are willing to be challenged?
- What needs to be in place from day one to intentionally cultivate a culture for engaging in tough work?
- On a daily basis, how will the opening of class prepare students for doing intellectually demanding work?
- How can transitions move students from one activity to another so that they stay tuned to learning?
- How will time be used?
- What will the ending of the class look and sound like?

Let's take a look at how Lesli and Emily began the year, then focus on the routines and rituals that set the stage for learning each day and that reflected their stance.

Setting the Stage at the Start of the Year

Lesli's plans for those first few days of school were simple yet elegant: "I want them to learn the routines and rituals of our classroom, but more important, I want them to reconnect to reading. If I can get them to remember a favorite moment, a happy time with a book, I have an opening for connecting them to literacy and I know that they'll get ready for the challenging work ahead of us. So I teach them our routines, but I keep our conversation focused on them and on building our classroom community."

On the first day of school, she introduced them to the daily ritual of "coming to the floor." Because she had arranged the desks in a horseshoe shape with several rows of desks partially circling the room, she had room in the center for students to sit on the floor. Bigger students or girls in dresses could choose to sit at one of the desks that were close to the center of the floor where the others sat sprawled out or cross-legged. Lesli sat facing them. At that point, she encouraged them to remember a time when they loved reading. For some students, it was a memory of a grandparent reading a picture book to them in bed at night while others remembered a book they read from the summer. The room was filled with stories and laugher.

This was Lesli's opportunity to introduce students to possible reads for the year. Along with hearing their stories, she talked about books that she loved and that they might fall in love with. Book talks filled her room during those first few weeks. She wanted to tease them with possibilities and open up options. Lesli was after two things at this point. First, she wanted to build community, which she did through the ritual of coming to the floor. Her stance that relationships matter in learning drove this routine, but her academic stance was also clear: "Our classroom is about reading and writing—each and every day. I want them to be clear about that."

Lesli's opening days were also dedicated to clarifying and practicing many of these daily routines. Because she knew that every second mattered, she showed students that their notebooks were stored on the shelf by the door and that their first task as they entered the room was to pick up the notebooks, check that they had something to read, and then move to their desks. When the bell rang they were to begin reading. And for those first few weeks, they practiced, practiced, practiced those opening moves.

Lesli continued to shape her routines and rituals by reflecting on both her vision and her stance. "I had to keep thinking hard about what I wanted to have happen in my classroom, and then I had to figure out what would make it happen." During the summer, she mulled over the previous year, identified rough spots, then determined what she needed to put in place in order to mitigate problems in the coming year. From that mulling over, she identified practices to ensure smoother transitions and better ways to clarify her goals or daily learning targets. She figured out more effective ways to informally assess students and ways to regularly celebrate their growth.

This reflective process highlights another aspect of Lesli's stance: she owned the responsibility for shaping the culture in the classroom. She could easily have reflected over the summer on how the students in the previous class had been particularly challenging and laughed at their foibles—which she, of course, did. But she didn't blame them. Instead, she thought about what was under her control and what she could do. Because Lesli's sense of agency was strong, she looked to herself to figure out what was under her sphere of influence and how to reshape the routines and rituals to strengthen her classroom culture.

Emily, too, worked from that stance of designing the kind of classroom culture where students could do tough intellectual work. From the moment her students walked into her room, Emily knew that she had to groom them to be novice scientists.

There's a particular way they talk to each other, a rhythm to the classroom, and a way to listen. And that's what she did those first few days of school: teach them how budding scientists act and think. "Because there's a lot of talk in my classroom, I have to make sure that everyone knows how to talk and how to listen." One of her district's charges is "accountable talk"—a kind of academic discourse in which students are accountable to their learning and the learning of others. Accountable talk requires students to listen carefully to each other, paraphrase the comments of their classmates, and respectfully challenge ideas, not individuals. In addition, speakers must be as accurate and specific as possible, using evidence and reasonable justification for their opinions. Even though many students had been in classrooms where accountable talk is the expected norm, Emily wanted to ensure that all knew what their scientific discourse would sound like.

One way that she incorporated accountable talk is through partner talk, one of her daily routines. As the year began, she explained the importance of students' turning to face their partner so that they could make eye contact. She taught them how to indicate listening through paraphrasing and then had them practice and practice that important skill. Some of this practice around how to talk focused on an important part of their science class: safety rules. She explained, "Each class needs to develop their own safety rules. I want everyone to take ownership of the rulemaking process for a couple of reasons. First, they need to understand the importance of those safety rules since we'll be doing labs throughout the year, and second, I want them to know how to be accountable in their talk, so that's what we work on." The topic of safety provided the means for her to build the kind of academic discourse that students would engage in throughout the school year.

Even though their content was different, the stance sitting under Lesli's and Emily's decisions during those first few days of teaching was similar. Unlike Marshall, who scared his students so they would be too afraid to misbehave, Lesli and Emily nurtured the kind of classroom community that would enable students to become smarter throughout the school year. Marshall, Lesli, and Emily might perform similar actions, such as setting norms for behavior and discussion, but because their stances differed, the way they implemented those actions differed vastly—and kids knew the difference.

Notice the similarities in both Emily and Lesli's stories. Those opening days are:

1. grounded in content, with Lesli focusing on literacy and Emily focusing on science
2. rich with discourse around a topic that frames the year (For Lesli, it's reconnecting to a time when they loved to read, and for Emily, it's about accountable talk and developing safety rules.)

3. open-ended explorations that encourage and even require multiple perspectives and voices
4. scaffolds for the year by leaving little to chance

Setting the Stage Daily

Having a routine for starting the class is probably one of the most common practices in America's classrooms. Teachers know that how they start class matters, and that if they lose students in the first few minutes, they'll have a difficult time catching their attention. What's important to consider, however, are the reasons behind a teacher's opening moves and the implications of the routines.

At one school where we've worked, teachers established a routine that's common to English classrooms across the nation: Daily Oral Language (DOL). In this practice, students begin class by correcting an error-filled sentence on the SMART Board. After a few minutes, the teachers lead the students through a discussion about their corrections. With the very best of intentions, those teachers justify the use of Daily Oral Language by explaining that their students struggle with editing and that DOL is one way of teaching correctness or that it is a way to prepare students for the yearly state assessment. But consider the implications of this routine: for about ten minutes (or more) each day, students study errors in writing. For a total of fifty minutes per week or two hundred minutes per month or up to 1,800 minutes per school year, students examine mistakes. And there is little payoff for this large investment of time. The students who walk into class knowing how to correct the error do well while the students who don't know the answer might gain a bit of knowledge about fixing errors. And what's the underpinning message? Writing is about correctness and fixing errors.

In other classes where we've worked, students walk into the room and check out the provocative quote the teacher has written on the board. For a little over five minutes, students copy the quote and respond to it while the teacher takes roll and hands back papers. Then they close their notebooks and begin the day's lesson. Again, with the best of intentions, the teachers explain that writing about quotes builds fluency. However, the question is, what happens to the journal writing at the end of those five minutes? In some of these classes, nothing. The response to the quote and the quote itself, disconnected from the work that follows, are like fuzzy dice dangling from a car's mirror: pure decoration and serving little purpose. What's the underpinning message? Other people have great ideas, and a student's job is to think about the message, not create it. This practice defines school as doing work that keeps a student quiet but leads nowhere. Such practices are simply fillers and are about compliance rather than engagement in vigorous, challenging ideas.

For Lesli and Emily, there was not a second of class time to waste; they planned and taught from a state of urgency. Too many of their students had a lot of catching up to do, so all routines had to count. If they wanted class to run like clockwork, they needed to figure out the structures that mattered.

For Emily, students had to be ready to think like scientists, which meant, in part, being focused on the day's goals. Their first task daily was to record the day's learning targets in their science notebooks and then respond in their journals to a Far Side cartoon. This attention to a cartoon may sound frivolous or unrelated, but Emily explained that what she was doing was building observational and inferential skills, both needed by scientists. As soon as Emily was through taking roll, she asked students to find a partner. Students found partners and began talking about their journal entries. Emily's typical routine was to listen in on their conversations and either acknowledge the good work they were doing or redirect them. It was not uncommon to hear her name what students were doing, such as, "I love how you're using other people's knowledge to get smarter."

For Lesli, the routine of reading every day at the start of the class prepared students to engage in the intellectual work ahead of them. They knew quite literally the second the class started that she would be conferring with someone. And what's the underpinning message behind this routine and ritual of reading a book of their choice? That reading matters. And the message sitting under the conferences? You can always grow and get even smarter as a reader. You can grow your skill by doing complex, challenging work.

Propping up every instructional decision was a clear purpose. As Lesli put it, "I don't care if they love reading. I don't care if they hate reading. I have a son who hates to read, so I get that. What I care about is that they know *how* to make meaning of print. They have to know what to do when they get difficult text and have to figure out what it means. This is a survival skill, not only for school but also for life. To achieve that, they need lots of time to read, and they need to know how to make sense out of what they read." Lesli's routines and rituals grew out of her stance that these students mattered and that her job was to build their confidence and solidify their skills. She worked from a sense of urgency and moral purpose. Following are routines from other teachers that demonstrate the effective use of class time.

Other Routines

Chuck Wolfram at Greenwood High School in Kentucky knows the importance of teaching from bell to bell and used to worry about how to do some of the required mundane routines at the start of class. The school required that teachers submit attendance reports to the office within the first five minutes. Because he didn't waste any time, he figured out a system where he could meet the requirement and get students into the work immediately.

Daily, one student was responsible for reviewing the previous day's lessons. When the bell rang, all the students would stand. The student responsible for the review would move to the front of the class facing the other students. This student would pose a question based on the previous day's work, call on a standing student, and then acknowledge whether the answer is correct or not. If correct, the student would sit down. This continued for about five minutes until most of the students were sitting and Chuck was ready to take over. Chuck's first move was to assign a student to be in charge of the review questions for the following day. With this very simple routine, students reviewed the previous day and Chuck completed his required duties and not a minute was wasted. The message was clear: students walk into his class to learn and to think.

Tami Wolff in Fort Collins, Colorado, uses a strategy similar to what we described in *Clock Watchers* (Quate and McDermott 2009). As she takes roll, she asks students a question about their personal life:

- What would you prefer: country music or hip-hop?
- What do you prefer: a board game or a video game?
- Who does your laundry?
- Madonna or Paris Hilton?
- Hot chocolate or chocolate milk?

What's important is her teaching stance: she believes that community is critical for students to learn, so the questions she asks are intended to build community by having students reveal a bit of themselves.

Tami also has been thoughtful about transitions. When one activity is about to end, she turns up the volume of the music quietly playing in the background, letting students know that it is time to move on.

Staying on the Stage

For a couple of years in Stevi's early days of teaching, the school district welcomed teachers back to school by gathering them into a large auditorium to hear an inspirational speaker. Her retention of those messages rarely lasted beyond the talk itself. Except for Harry Wong's. Even though it's decades later, she can still hear Harry Wong cajole the teachers into never working harder than their students. "At the end of the day, they should walk out of school exhausted and you should walk out energized."

To do that, though, teachers must not only set the stage for learning but also create the conditions that will get kids on the stage and keep the spotlight on them. It means students must be the workers, as Ted Sizer reminds us in *Horace's Compromise* (2004), and it means making the mantra "whoever is doing the working is doing the learning" a reality.

If we want to challenge students in a way that keeps them on the stage, then once again, we can learn from Lesli and Emily and other teachers. We can learn how they organize the limited classroom time they have with students, how they check in with students on a regular basis to ensure that the challenge is appropriate and that students are growing, and how they ensure that all student voices are a part of the ongoing classroom discourse.

Organizing Time: The Workshop Model of Instruction

Lesli had carefully thought about how to use that precious commodity, time, in order to meet her overarching goal of having students confidently meet academic challenges. She needed to figure out how students would have the time to delve deeply into thinking and, at the same time, receive the explicit instruction that would lead to success. Informed by the work of Samantha Bennett (2007), the framework she used was the workshop model of instruction. Daily, she made sure that three major routines followed independent reading: a minilesson, work time, and a debrief. The workshop model of instruction, also called studio workshop (Kirby and Kirby 2007), is based on a simple principle, well known in the artisan community: to actually do important work requires a large chunk of time. In other words, Lesli's classroom was not one where she was front and center most of the time. Instead, she provided just enough instruction so that students could do the work—the spotlight would be shining on them.

The Opening and the Minilesson

Lesli's opening was her routine of independent reading discussed earlier. During these opening moments, some teachers take roll and handle those bureaucratic necessities. Lesli had deliberately decided to handle those tasks at other times during class. Instead, she wanted to use this time to confer with students.

The next routine, the minilesson, included a change in seating arrangements as students moved to the floor. There she taught them how to do the thinking that would lead to success with the academic work of the day. Sitting cross-legged on the floor, she navigated between modeling the thinking she wanted students to do, annotating text or generating notes on the document camera, and engaging in a focused discussion.

This ritual of moving to the floor was intentional for building community and marking a transition—from silent reading to whole-class instruction. Lesli explained the importance of having students sit on the floor or move the desks in close to the rest of the class. "When we sit together, we become a tighter community than when we stay at our desks. It's hard to poke fun of someone who is sitting right next to you. When you can feel their pain, you're nicer. At the same time, it's a physical challenge for some of my students, especially the boys, so I give them a choice of sitting at a desk but staying close to us or scooting down on the floor."

Too often, workshop is seen as an appropriate instructional model solely for the language arts classroom, where students are engaged in reading or writing. But Emily sees it as the ideal way to organize her science classroom. Like Lesli, after her opening routine, she moves students to the floor for a minilesson. Often her minilesson includes probing questions that help her understand how student thinking is evolving as well as model her thinking through a "think-aloud." Read how the first few minutes of workshop looked and sounded in Emily's science classroom:

A few minutes after class began, Emily checked that the students had finished their work on the opening routine of recording their learning targets in their science notebooks and jotting down observations about the Far Side cartoon. For the last few days, they had worked on sharpening their observation skills and using their background knowledge to make sense of their observations. Since she believed that students often know more than what they think they do, she wanted to show them that they could solve many problems by applying their background knowledge. Today she planned to move them forward to show them how to do this, but first she wanted to check in on their observational skills (see Figure 2.2).

Since most students seemed finished with their opening work, she moved them quickly to the front of the room and began the day's minilesson, "One, two, three, go! Thumbs up if you're with me. I'm going to start with Carlie. What's your observation?" As students discussed the cartoon, she named the intellectual moves students were making, moves that she wanted to become habitual: "I love how some of you are using the scientific vocabulary that we've been working on this week."

Confident that students were growing in their observational and inferential skills, Emily shifted gears. "Take a look at your learning target for today. We're going to go deeper as we think like scientists. Today we're going to look at how our background knowledge helps us understand a difficult scientific concept. Let me show you how

Figure 2.2: Graphic Organizer

I observed	My background knowledge is	Therefore . . .

I do this, and then I'm going to ask you to do the same thing. I'm going to play this video and stop it every now and then to show you my thinking. Remember, this is the same kind of thinking that I'll ask you to do."

Emily turned on the video and, after a few minutes, stopped it and began to narrate her thinking. "When I hear this comment about atoms or Adams, my brain goes in two directions: Addams Family or the atom bomb. I'm not a genius on this, but I'm betting it has something to do with an atom. He even used a word that I'm not sure is even a word: *un-break-apart-able*. There are four different pieces here, which makes me think about what else we might now be able to break apart." She paused and looked at one of the students. "So, Jessica, that goes back to your question. What is an atom? That word makes me think about . . ." then continued narrating her thinking, making connections to discussions they had had in class and noting other connections. As she talked, she began to build a picture that made the concept of an atom come to life. After a couple of minutes, she turned to the students and said, "I challenge you to write one sentence that shows your thinking. That sentence has to include your background knowledge and how that connection helped you understand the ideas in this upcoming segment. You'll work with the person next to you. So in two minutes, make sure that sentence is written."

At the end of the two minutes, she checked in. Pleased with what she heard, she asked them to return to their seats to continue this kind of thinking on the rest of the video.

Work Time

In both Lesli's and Emily's classrooms, the majority of time was devoted to shaping students as workers rather than as passive consumers of information. Students talked, they argued, they read, they wrote, and they learned. Sometimes they worked in groups and sometimes they worked independently. Lesli's and Emily's role was to coach them to be successful, but the students were doing the heavy lifting of intellectual work for that day.

Reflection

Both Emily and Lesli ended class by having students reflect on their thinking and learning of the day. This routine was easy to lose, but they had found ways to keep this time sacred. Some teachers new to the workshop model use timers as reminders to save these last few minutes for reflection while others ask a student to monitor time and send a hand signal for when it's time to ponder how the day went.

For Lesli, the ending of the day often included a review of the learning target. How close were students to meeting that target? What else did they need in order to meet that target? Some days she asked random students to respond to those closing questions, and some days she asked students to write an exit card with a comment about what they had learned or questions that they still needed answered (see Figure 2.3).

Figure 2.3: Exit Slip from Lesli's Student

Monday Learning Targets	Formative Assessment	Calendar
I can identify the perspective of a piece of text.	1　2　3　④　5	It's hard to tell the difference when we do it in the same day.
I can identify point of view.	1　②　3　4　5	

Tuesday Learning Targets	Formative Assessment	Calendar
I can identify perspective.	1　2　3　④　5	This was easier.
I can use a comma in an introductory clause.	1　2　③　4　5	

Wednesday Learning Targets	Formative Assessment	Calendar
I can identify point of view.	1　2　③　4　5	I'm still confused between 2nd and 3rd. This is easy.
I can use commas in a list.	1　2　3　4　⑤	

Emily's reflections at the end of each day provided information that helped her plan the next day's lesson. "Often in these debriefs, I have them tell me what they need next to know. For instance, as they're learning about reliable data, I might ask them how they would know if their data is reliable and what help they need. The responses are always fascinating. Just the other day a student responded that it would be helpful to see what other scientists were thinking. From that reflection, I knew the student was valuing modeling and was beginning to see himself as a scientist." Pretty cool, don't you think?

Formative Assessment Through Conferring

Because Lesli had structured her classroom like a workshop, she had routines that enabled her to formatively assess students on the spot. For her, there's not a better way to determine if students are being appropriately challenged—and supported in meeting the challenge. As we saw in Chapter 1, when students were reading their novels, her role was to confer. These conferences let her inside each student's head to learn how each was progressing and what instruction would be most important at that specific moment: "I need to be able to teach students how to navigate the world of print. That's what I'm doing when I confer. I'm teaching the individual about thinking while reading." At the same time, students sitting nearby were eavesdropping. "This gives me a sneaky way to teach several students a specific skill. I know that others are listening, and I want to make sure that what I teach also applies to others."

Even though the students didn't know it, Lesli had carefully mapped out where students sat. Using data from the state and district assessments, Lesli developed her seating chart so that students with different proficiency levels sat next to each other. She knew which students needed the most support and, during the conferring, made certain to touch base with them a bit more often.

"In my conferences," she explained, "I can give students that just-in-time feedback that they need to move forward. If I didn't have an expedient way of seating kids, I'm afraid I'd either ignore those who most need my help or waste time daily figuring out whom to see next." With each conference and each teaching point that addressed a student's immediate need, she developed their skill set and readied them for a greater challenge.

During work time, Emily conferred with students on a regular basis. Often her conferring was with a group of students rather than an individual. By carefully monitoring how each group was progressing, she made sure that they received the on-the-spot and just-in-time guidance that would increase their readiness to take on challenging work. Also, like Lesli, she is strategic about whom she conferred with and mapped out each day which groups to see. Typically, though, she was able to touch base with each group.

This was a relatively new practice that Emily added to her teaching repertoire. Even though she had always monitored student work time, her stance that year shifted. Instead of focusing on on-task behavior, she focused on probing their thinking. "I'm learning to pose questions to understand how they're thinking. Then, when I have an idea about each person's thought process, I provide descriptive feedback or I do a little more modeling. I try hard not to give them answers. After all, I want them to know they can do the thinking and that I'm not a crutch."

This shift in stance and refinement of practice has paid off. Each year the district surveys students to learn about their perceptions of the level of challenge in their classes. Emily always rates high, but along with that high rating, students acknowledge that they are supported in meeting the challenge. In their exit cards, students frequently comment on how she pushed their thinking: "You ask us questions and you won't let us leave if we don't know."

All Means All: Discourse Protocols

Formative assessment practices such as conferring let the teacher know if the level of challenge is appropriate and, therefore, whether students are center stage; additionally, it's a way for teachers to be certain they are supporting student growth.

But nothing seems much easier than using student discourse as a way to check in on student thinking. In *Opening Minds* (2012) Peter Johnston reminds the reader about the importance of discourse in learning. Describing "dialogical classrooms," where students are engaged in robust talk, Johnston notes that student achievement in such classrooms increased while the achievement gap decreased. He comments: "Given these benefits, and the sheer fun of it for teachers and students, you would think that dialogue would be rampant in classrooms across the country. Alas, it is not (53)."

Check this out! Research by Martin Nystrand (1997) shows that students in eighth-grade English classrooms across the nation are engaged in dialogue fifty seconds a day. Yes, that's seconds! And ninth grade? Fifteen seconds!

This is not the case in the classrooms we've studied, where students were engaged through challenge. In those classes, talk was an important daily classroom routine. Students were not only deeply engaged in learning but actually having fun doing challenging work. These teachers structured this talk in various ways. Lesli, for example, encouraged students simply to talk and to stop raising their hands. "This is how adults talk, and you're learning to talk like smart adults in here, so just speak up and don't raise your hands." Of course, she had to remind them how to listen to each other and to make sure that they didn't interrupt. Even in the teacher-focused portion of the workshop, Emily made sure that students had multiple opportunities to talk. Peppered throughout her minilessons were invitations for students to turn and talk to a partner. Often at the start of her minilessons, she would position them to be ready to talk: "Please find one person sitting next to you and sit face to face." Emily monitored this carefully to make sure that each student in the class was talking to someone and that no one in the pair dominated the discussion.

For this to happen, students had to have something to talk about. Emily often used what she called "think questions"—open-ended, provocative questions about meaty topics. In Lesli's class, students wrestled with essential questions that guided the unit and sometimes the year. For instance, Lesli's question for one unit was "Where does your right to develop and express your unique identity end and the rights of others who would object begin?" This question invited conversation not only from her eighth graders but also from Steve, the custodian. One day Lesli found this message from him on her desk:

> Lesli,
> If there is an answer for the question please let me know what it is. I thought <u>what a question</u>. There's always been at least one person in every situation I've been in that just makes it a mission to break my spirit. Good question.
> —Steve

Alisa Wills-Keely, a high school teacher in the Denver area, designed her lessons so that students wrestled with both essential questions and topical questions. Essential questions framed the unit while topical questions were specific to the day's lesson. For instance, her essential question for a unit on *Les Miserables* was "How can one transcend or escape his/her past?" She compared the unit's essential question to the centerpiece at a dinner party, something that reflected the theme of the party and that everyone could speak to at the table. Her hope for the question was that kids could wake up in the morning and be excited to talk about it during the day. Topical questions, on the other hand, drove the thinking for the day's workshop. For instance, on the day that students were analyzing Victor Hugo's style and then revising their own writing, her topical question was "What choices do authors make that cause you to react, think, and feel?"

As Alisa conferred with groups or led a class discussion, her invitations to talk were clear:

- And who else has a question about this?
- Who sees this differently?
- How else do we know that data is valid and reliable?
- I wonder if there's another way that we could think about this.
- Tell me more about that.
- Let's think about it from another angle. Who can start us off?
- What difference does this make? And what's another difference?

Along with asking questions, these teachers nurtured their students' readiness to engage in these often animated discussions, thereby creating access to greater intellectual challenges. Remember the interchange between Lesli and Jerardo in Chapter 1? "Come on, Jerardo. Fight with me." Playfully, Lesli welcomed Jerardo into the discussion to add a new perspective, one that differed from hers. Emily may not have asked students to fight with her, but she pushed them to voice alternate opinions and then to defend their positions.

Alisa uses a different kind of routine and ritual to build student readiness to engage in discourse. Frequently she will use protocols to guide small-group discussions. "I want all students' voices to be a part of our discussions, and I mean all, not just a few." When she uses a protocol, she knows that the shy students will participate and that the highly vocal students will not dominate the air space. Early in the school year, Alisa worked with her students on how to be productive in small groups and introduced them to protocols.

On the day that students were working on revising their writing, the protocol was simple. Each student was given a stack of different-color sticky notes. Silently, they

Figure 2.4: Sticky Note Protocol

Sticky Note Protocol

1. Select your color of sticky notes. Each person should have a different color.
2. Read each paper and respond to the content, but avoid editing right now:
   a. Note lines you liked.
   b. Jot down questions you have.
   c. Indicate confusions.
   d. Point out images or metaphors that work well.
3. When you finish one paper, pass it on to the next person.
4. Once you have commented on each paper, read the comments on your paper.
5. Then focus on one paper at a time. Begin with the person who most recently had a birthday.
6. The writer guides the conversation by responding to the stickies. Ideas for response:
   a. What are you thinking about now after reading your group's responses?
   b. What sticky comments confused you? What do you want to know more about?
   c. What might you do next? What does your group think about that step?
7. The writer makes a commitment to next steps in the revision process.
8. The process continues with the writer to the left.

read each other's papers and on the stickies jotted down observations and questions, including places where they were moved and spots in the work where they were confused. Only after they had responded to each of the papers did they talk, in an orderly manner, about one paper at a time. As writers read the comments, they posed questions and asked for elaboration. Or they suggested possible revisions and asked for reactions from their group members (see Figure 2.4 and, for more protocols to guide discussion of text, see the appendix).

Let's talk about the obvious: what's the connection between the routine and ritual of discourse and challenge? If there's nothing to talk about, nothing to wrestle with, nothing to explore, where's the challenge? How will students be engaged? And what's the point of the work if there's nothing to think about?

Routines and Rituals: A Final Thought

Routines and rituals can seem almost sacred to us; they make us feel secure; they are predictable, safe, and familiar. And when those routines and rituals are designed to lead students to do ever-smarter, more challenging work, the classroom can sing.

And the difference well-designed rituals and routines make in a teacher can be invigorating. Time and time again we saw Lesli and Emily moved by the work that their students do. "I just love my job," Emily said one day, tears in the corners of her eyes.

And her students love being there.

Reflection

DEFINING A VISION AND MAKING IT A REALITY

Defining a Vision

What are my hopes and dreams for my students? What beliefs about my content area do I want them to have? What attitudes do I want to foster? What skills do I want them to have?

Thinking Through Potential Challenges

What routines and rituals do I want to have in place so that my classroom becomes a place for students to think deeply and so that my vision becomes a reality?

Routine/Ritual	How does it build my vision?	What's the payoff for students?

Setting the Stage

What do I need to do during the first day of class in order to set the stage for the year's work?

What do students need to do at the start of each class so that they are ready to begin doing smart, intellectual work?

Window into Practice: After

As you read the following vignette describing Mrs. Green a few months after the vignette that opened Part 1 on teacher stance, what do you notice about her stance? What evidence is there that it's changed? Consider her language, the room arrangement, and the work that the students are doing.

When students ambled into Mrs. Green's classroom that spring, they no longer sat in rows. Instead, the students were in a circle. For this particular day, Mrs. Green was outside the circle.

"I'm betting you're all ready to talk about *The Giver*. Yesterday it looked as though you had gathered quite a few notes for the seminar, so let's get started. Michael, would you remind us of the norms for a seminar?"

"We can't interrupt each other and we have to use evidence from the books. Is that right?" He looked at her for approval.

"Jonathan, what do you think? Would you help Michael out?"

"We have to listen to each other too, and we can't talk too much. We have to share the airspace."

"And who's going to start?" Mrs. Green asked.

As Michael kicked off the discussion, Mrs. Green sat down behind her desk and listened. She noted that the students stayed grounded in the book and explored issues within this novel.

She smiled and nodded in approval, pleased that they were engaging in text better than they had all year. She knew that her work at providing strategies to support their thinking was working and was pleased that she was able to shift her stance from a rescuer to a caretaker of their intellects. It had been hard work on her part and hard on their part since they were used to her doing a good share of the intellectual work for them. But they were having fun and trusting that they could actually do the thinking.

The Nature of the Work

Window into Practice: Before

As you read this vignette, think about the nature of the work that Mr. Lynne assigned his students. What do you notice about that work and its level of challenge? What is there about the work that motivates and engages—or doesn't motivate and engage—students? At the end of Part 2, you'll return to his classroom to see what changes occurred after he learned more about the nature of the work that challenges and engages students.

"Do you remember how to story-map? We did that the other day," Mr. Lynne asked his students.

Several kids nodded affirmatively. As he walked around the room handing a blank story map to each group, he reminded them. "Open your books to 'The Gift of the Magi,' and then see if you can figure out the exposition and . . ."

Two students at one table quickly opened their books. Without a word passing between them, they worked through the first story map. After a minute or two, the girl looked up. "I think the exposition included how they wanted to buy presents for each other but were too poor to afford the gift." Her partner nodded, and they continued.

At the table next to the two of them, a couple of boys were deep in discussion about pimples. "You should have seen what happened when I squeezed this pimple last night. It was something else." Soon the two boys were trying to out-gross each other with graphic details.

Mr. Lynne wandered over to their table. "You remember what exposition is?" He explained to them while they politely listened, not telling him that they had nearly completed their map. After Mr. Lynne moved on to another group, the boys continued telling pimple stories as the group of four filled in their story maps.

"Remember when we did this is seventh grade?" one boy asked his tablemate.

"I think so," she said, as she put her completed story map into her folder.

"When you're done, get your vocabulary cards out and then copy the words at the bottom of the story onto each card."

The students complied, and the pimple conversation continued as they looked through "The Gift of the Magi," copying the three or four words at the bottom of each page onto their index cards with the definitions.

> The fundamental challenge is to create a set of circumstances in which students take pleasure in learning and come to believe that the information and skills they are being asked to learn are important . . . and worth their effort. —**National Research Council, Engaging Schools**

CHAPTER 3

Work That Matters over Time

Teacher in the Spotlight

Jennifer Reinert is a math teacher at a Denver high school.

Jennifer Reinert described her Algebra 2 class. "I have forty students in my classroom, and on most days thirty-eight of them show up." Sounds like good news: students are actually attending her high school math class and this in a school not known for stellar attendance. "However, I only have twenty-eight desks in the room," Jennifer said laughing.

This is one among many problems faced by Jennifer, a third-year math teacher. "Fifty percent of this class is inclusion, so half are students with special needs while the other 50 percent includes highly skilled and moderately skilled math students. I have students who read at a second-grade level and who literally cannot add. So I have a wide spectrum of ability levels in my classes."

Jennifer continued, "With severe cutbacks in funding, many of our teachers face what appear to be insurmountable odds as they try to engage students in learning. We also have some very vibrant and vocal students who destroy the flow of the lesson. It takes considerable time to get the class back after these disruptions." In addition, some students are convinced that school is not a place for them since they've experienced little success and tremendous failure. "What's this have to do with me?" is a common refrain. Why should they try?

Yet despite these challenges, Jennifer's teaching stance is clear: with support, her students will grow as mathematicians. Willing to work as hard as she can to make a difference in their lives, she offers challenging work to her students and remains optimistic that she can make a difference in their lives. Of course, we wouldn't be writing about Jennifer if she hadn't been successful. It wasn't accidental that Jennifer was able to hook and move this typically disengaged group. As she reflected on how she could engage students in the math, she explained how she had to be deliberate about the nature of the work she offered her students. Jennifer knew that she had to design work that was tied to the standards, that mattered to them, and that could counteract their attitude that school wasn't for them.

Conversation About Common Core: The Nature of the Work

Stevi and John take a closer look at the nature of the work related to the Common Core State Standards.

John: What we write about is what they are talking about in the CCSS: higher-order thinking, comparing, contrasting, analyzing, creating, and problem solving.

Stevi: I think what we have added is the transformation piece. We add the "Why does it matter to the student?" element that is often missing in the curriculum.

John: We go back once again to the idea that if it doesn't matter to the students, it simply doesn't matter.

Stevi: Teachers could take a topic, make it local and make it really matter. There are lots of ways to play with content if you keep in mind that being local can motivate and engage learners. I think about what Jennifer said. She talks to colleagues all the time about "How can I make this math concept matter to my students?"

John: I think what we are showing here is that the intentional commitment to higher-order thinking is not only a unit focus but a daily commitment to make the connections to students' lives and communities. It is the intimate relationship among the academic press, transformative teaching, and authentic work that allows students to deeply understand the focus of the learning.

Strategy 4: Make the Work Call for Academic Press

John didn't have the same kind of challenges that Jennifer did, but he too faced challenges throughout his career. In 1983 when teaching a seventh-grade social studies class, he overheard his students discussing how boring history had been. He can still hear one student's statement: "All the teacher does is talk at us; I would rather be in bed." John didn't think he was boring; in fact, he was certain that he was entertaining because of his theatrical presence in the classroom. However, when his principal watched him teach, the principal agreed with the students. "You are an entertaining teacher, but you're doing all the work. You have no clue what your students have learned." John was shaken, especially when he realized that the principal was right. John was doing all the talking and, therefore, all the learning. As he planned, he had focused on what content *he* was going to deliver and how *he* would teach that content in an entertaining manner, but he hadn't focused on engaging the students in the learning. He hadn't thought enough about the nature of the work that would challenge students and allow them to grow.

With nudging from his principal, John agreed to attend a workshop on developing relevant problem-solving curriculum. The complicated but intellectually stimulating series of steps required students to think hard about real-world problems. The facilitators of the workshop insisted that the students had to do the work and the teacher had to coach. John was hearing the call for academic press.

Academic press refers to a classroom and school environment designed to engage students in critical thinking. The term *press* is intentional; the curriculum, the teacher, the tasks, and the environment all press the student to understand the importance and value of thinking and thinking hard. Shouse (1996) argues that academic press is about creating an academic climate where depth of understanding is the goal and where students perceive the importance of that goal. It's this press for understanding that demands higher-order thinking skills (National Research Council 2004; Middleton 2009). Academic press pushes up against compliance or grade grubbing. Instead of shooting for a grade, students work toward understanding important concepts where they link prior knowledge to new knowledge in order to solve problems and justify their thinking. Students see the importance of the work itself and are willing to participate with "minds on." Academic press is an integral element of challenging work that requires students to analyze, interpret, evaluate, and problem-solve, all within a real-world context.

John left the workshop energized. Hoping he could capture his students' hearts and minds as they were doing the work of complex thinking, he could not wait to try out the strategies with his novice historians. Still he wasn't sure how his students would actually respond. Would they be willing to work with "minds on"? Could he find the real-world problem that led students to engagement and not mere compliance? How would they respond to this call for academic press?

In the news that fall was the perfect situation to push his students academically. President Reagan had placed peacekeeping troops in Beirut, Lebanon, during the tumultuous Lebanese Civil War. John knew this current event would lend itself well to academic press. It was perfect for pressing students to:

1. analyze data,
2. interpret facts,
3. apply the information to a new situation,
4. predict what would happen in the future,
5. evaluate the probability that their prediction might happen, and
6. create possible solutions to the problem.

In other words, students would be doing the thinking of historians, political advisors, and members of think tanks in Washington, DC.

John introduced the unit with a quote from Fredrick Douglass: "Without a struggle, there can be no progress, so get ready to struggle!" Then John told his students they would be doing the work of advisors to the President. He saw his students sit up straighter and lean forward at their desks. He explained one of their culminating tasks: "You can send your ideas to the President and his cabinet in a letter; who knows, maybe they will listen to you."

The students set to work gathering facts concerning previous events in the Middle East. Then the students investigated the facts around the current situation involving our peacekeeping troops. Next, they analyzed and interpreted the similarities and differences between previous events and what was occurring at that time. Yes, the students were doing the thinking and the talking and were totally engaged in the struggle of challenging academic work. They had to apply the newly found information to the situation in Beirut, make predictions concerning what would happen to our troops in Lebanon, and evaluate the likelihood of their prediction coming true. Finally, they had to creatively sell their ideas to the government through a convincing letter addressed to their local congressman. This was academic press!

As their hard work neared its end, the students were excited to share their predictions and solutions. From their investigation of probable outcomes in Lebanon, this seventh-grade class had come to the conclusion that our troops were in grave danger and that many casualties could result from their deployment. The United States had to get out of Beirut.

Their excitement turned sour on October 23, 1983. A suicide bomber killed 299 U.S. troops stationed in Lebanon. John and his students were stunned and angry. One student questioned, "If a bunch of seventh graders could figure this out, why can't the President and his cabinet figure it out?"

Emotions ran high and the learning ran deep. John had the privilege of facilitating this dynamic classroom filled with excited, curious students, often working out of their comfort zone. He no longer had to be the entertaining teacher; instead, the students kept pressing and pressing as they built their understanding about the event and recognized the need to know history. Nearly thirty years later, the thinking of this group of seventh graders still stands out among the thousands of classes John has taught. John and his students learned a great deal that day about the power of hard work; if pressed, students can think—and want to think—at high levels.

Jennifer's Press

Like John and his seventh graders, Jennifer wasn't satisfied with the standard plans for teaching math concepts to her students. She wanted her apprentice mathematicians to think and work hard, so academic press was important to her as she planned and revised her unit. "Since we were in the probability unit, we were talking about simple probabilities, such as flipping a coin or rolling a die, not really 'real-life' stuff." Jennifer couldn't help but notice her students' lackluster response to these mundane exercises. Some students were in the mode of compliance while others barely kept their eyes open. "I knew I had to do something to hook them and get them involved more deeply in the work and thinking." At that point in the unit, there was little academic press.

As she thought about what she needed to do, she recalled a conference session she had attended. Two teachers modeled an investigation of race and traffic violations. This work grabbed Jennifer's attention, and she wondered how she could duplicate this level of thinking in her probability unit. Then it popped into her head. Why not look at suspensions in her school? She knew about the research on race and suspensions:

> Although our national discourse on racial disparity tends to focus on academic outcomes—the so-called achievement gap—in school districts throughout the United States, Black, Latino, and American Indian students are also subject to a differential and disproportionate rate of school disciplinary sanctions, ranging from office disciplinary referrals to corporal punishment, suspension, and expulsion. (Gregory, Skiba, and Noguera 2010, 59)

She had watched many of her students miss class due to suspensions, so she knew this was an issue that touched them and could bring the concept of probability to life.

"I wanted them to look at the disproportionate number of high school suspensions involving minority males, not only in the American school system but in *our* high school." Jennifer thought about how deeply she could delve into this concept. She wanted her students to analyze and interpret data, and she needed them to make predictions as they applied the learning to their lives. Her students would gain insights into themselves through this unit as they evaluated their relationship to the data and possibly create new possibilities for how they would interact in the world. On top of that, she wanted the work to be inviting so that students would actually want to think and work hard. In other words, Jennifer focused on an essential support: the academic press.

As she thought about using the data on suspensions in her probability unit, she got excited and contacted the assistant principal, Caroline Gaudiani—Ms. G, as her students called her—to get her hands on the discipline data for her high school. The perfect partner for this challenging work, Mrs. G knew the name and situation of every student in the building. Together they planned and taught the unit.

If her goal was to understand the concept of probability, Jennifer needed to use this content to challenge her students to analyze and interpret the data. As Wiggins and McTighe assert, "merely giving back on tests the official theory of the textbook or the teacher is not evidence of understanding. We need to explain why our answer is correct, why the fact exists, why the formula works; we need to supply support for our opinions" (2005, 87). Jennifer's inclusion of her high school's data on suspensions offered her students the opportunity to evaluate what was happening in their community.

The high school statistics around suspensions had immediate application to Jennifer's students. Jennifer knew when the students in her class saw the reality of their role in these statistics, they would apply the information to their lived experience.

Realizing the need to press her students, Jennifer revised the learning activities in her unit, keeping focused on the goal of students understanding probability. As the students proceeded through the lesson, they evaluated the high school suspension data from multiple perspectives and considered new possibilities for the black, male, poverty-stricken, and special education students at their school. Because Ms. G co-planned and co-taught, she listened to students' advice for policy revisions.

Jennifer chose a topic that motivated students to gain self-knowledge. Often overlooked, self-knowledge takes learning and makes it personal. When students in Jennifer's classroom thought about how the information affected each and every one of them, they were able to predict how the data would play out in their lives with the hope of adjusting their behavior accordingly. "Self-knowledge is a key facet of understanding because it demands that we self-consciously question our ways of seeing the world if we are to become more understanding—better able to see beyond ourselves" (Wiggins and McTighe 2005, 102).

Jennifer's students, like John's, became engaged and emotionally attached to their learning. This result is not surprising. The National Research Council noted the relationship between challenge and higher-order thinking: "observers' ratings of the level of challenge and the degree to which higher-order thinking was required in classes were strongly correlated to their ratings of student engagement" (2004, 50). When teachers purposely include academic press in their planning, they create the conditions for students to experience the satisfaction that hard work though higher-level thinking can bring. They turn up the volume of student voice. This increases the likelihood that teachers will hear how brilliant their students really are.

Strategy 5: Provide Work That Is Transformative

Jennifer knew that the work that students do must matter. The work needs to reach in and grab the heart and soul and brain of the learner. It can't be ordinary, mundane, or disconnected from the world around them. Fundamentally, the nature of the work must connect to the world the students live in and help them figure out an answer to these questions: Why does this work matter? How will this work help me figure out my place in the world?

In other words, the essential nature of work that challenges and engages is transformative. If the work doesn't connect with the learner, then it doesn't have the power to transform or change them. According to James Banks, transformation occurs when "the structure of the curriculum is changed to enable students to view concepts, issues, events, and themes from the perspective of diverse ethnic and cultural groups" (Wink 2011, 32). All of us have a touch of egocentricity, and we know that's a prevailing characteristic of teens. Transformative work builds on that sense of self, answering the question of why this work matters to me.

We're not talking here about some of the superficial work that has happened under the umbrella of cultural diversity. No, we're not talking about just celebrating cultural heroes or holidays like Martin Luther King, Jr., Day or months dedicated to black history. Transformative work goes well beyond concepts or themes that are sometimes clumsily added to the curriculum. Instead, transformative work integrates community and cultural issues into daily life in the schoolroom. With a bridge from the world they know outside of school to the world within the classroom, student learning can be enhanced (Wilhelm 2007; Wink 2011).

In *Drive* (2009), Daniel Pink explores the research on motivation. His subtitle captures his thesis: *The Surprising Truth About What Motivates Us*. Often what we think will motivate people isn't the answer. In the world of work, money is often considered the motivator, but Pink found that after a point money wasn't an effective enticement. In schools, many teachers believe that grades are what motivate students, particularly, high school students, who, teachers fear, would resist doing work without a grade attached to it. Pink's reading of the research would push back against that belief. Purpose, he argues, is critical if people are working at high levels: "The most deeply motivated people—not to mention those who are most productive and satisfied—hitch their desires to a cause larger than themselves" (133). He continues, "From the moment that human beings first stared into the sky, contemplated their place in the universe, and tried to create something that bettered the world and outlasted their lives, we have been purpose seekers" (134). Transformative work provides that purpose while at the same time meeting the criteria of relevance. Transformative work is work that matters.

A teacher, such as Jennifer, knows that an important of element of the work she assigns is that students must find a purpose in the work and see how it connects to their lives. To do this Jennifer needs to know where her students live, what the local issues are, and what her students believe in. Wink (2011) states:

> The transformation approach includes complex ethnic issues and subject matters from a multi-perspective view. . . . Content is learned from the perspective of the non-dominant groups as well as the dominant group. This approach unifies many perspectives and creates a larger one. (33)

Jennifer knew well that if the work she assigned students didn't matter to them and if they couldn't see themselves and their community in the lesson, she could exert all the effort she wanted, but it would go nowhere. She would be exerting the effort, not the students. She would understand the purpose of the work, but they wouldn't. She understood that mathematical concepts devoid of connection to students' lives could easily fade into a drone of background noise.

Getting Grounded in the Community

Dr. Antwan Jefferson, a University of Colorado at Denver professor, has extensively studied transformative teaching. This approach to teaching requires the teacher to view school through a community and cultural lens. "It is very much like my family, I share blood with them, but I also share values with them, I share time and stories with them. I've built a history with them, a timeline or a chronology of my life. The development of my identity as a human being is connected to my family. The development of my identity as a professional is connected to a community."

In an interview, Antwan clarified the concept of transformative teaching:

> I am not referring to being a community-aware teacher or a community-connected teacher. Community-aware means knowing where the boundaries are, what the resources are, and how the local chamber of commerce website describes the community. A community-connected teacher is a teacher who can say, I've been to the boys and girls club and I know who the director is. I've been to the library and I send my students there. However, there is a different stance about being an educator in the community, and for now, I would describe that as being community-grounded, meaning, my feet are in the community; I'm planted and belong to this community.

How can a teacher find the time to be grounded in the community? The job is already overwhelming and a teacher deserves to have a life. According to Antwan, this grounding is a natural process. "I see where my students hang out, and I drop by to talk with them. If I see them outside their house, I drop by to meet their parents. I make it a point to talk to, listen to, and laugh with my students. Yes, knowing the physical assets of the community is important, but my students don't hang out at many of these places; I need to show up where my students are when the opportunity presents itself."

Jennifer understood Antwan's emphasis on being community-grounded. Even though she doesn't live in the neighborhood surrounding the school, she listens to the students' stories of how they spend time before and after school. She occasionally drops by some of the neighborhood parks and rec centers where her students are shooting hoops. When the school invites the community to participate in a local event, Jennifer is right there, getting to know the parents and the community leaders. She sees herself as planted within the community and makes every effort to greet parents at the homecoming picnic and at the music festival in a park near the school. Because she knows the community, she is better able to find the entry points for students to find themselves within the math curriculum. Figure 3.1 suggests one way to become community-grounded.

Planning for the Transformative Lesson or Unit

Jennifer works hard at figuring out transformative lessons connected to the community. Even though this is a consideration early in her unit plans, she often finds that the transformative lessons occur toward the end of the unit. She explains:

> The actual planning of these lessons usually takes a large amount of time and requires me to seek outside resources. I think about transformative lessons all through the unit, ask colleagues if they have resources, do many Internet searches, and then get the lessons put together much further into the unit. So

Figure 3.1: Community Assets Map

> ## The Community Assets Map
>
> The assets map is for discovering the assets in the community. Here's how it works.
>
> 1. The teacher's job is to discover the assets of the local and school community and make these assets a part of their students' educational experience. What are the local community organizations that support students and their families? What role do the local religious organizations play in the community? What are the best parks in the area? What are the local cultural celebrations? What are the best restaurants in the area? What are the local charitable institutions? You get the idea.
> 2. Go to these places, meet the people, and ask how they would like to be involved in the education of the students. Find out which students frequent which organization, and make it a point to ask about their experiences. Bring these assets into your curriculum.

planning transformative lessons begins early, but the actual execution of them tends to occur near the end of the unit. At the end of the unit, I can really incorporate all of the skills we learned into this activity and show the kids the relevance of what we have been doing.

Always clear about the unit's learning targets, Jennifer reshapes the learning activities as she moves through the unit, making sure that both academic press and transformation are key elements.

Planning transformative lessons may seem overwhelming at first. After all, synthesizing community and content is far from easy. It requires the teacher to engage in the highest levels of critical thinking. Along with knowing the community, the teacher must analyze the required curriculum to find points where students can enter into the learning (see Figure 3.2). In *Five Standards for Effective Teaching*, Stephanie Dalton states:

> Teachers can use the learning context to affirm and value students' backgrounds and to create common reference points for learning. They can prepare learning experiences in contexts sufficiently robust to provide knowledge that students can use in new situations. Such pedagogy links school, home, and community. (2007, 27)

Transformative learning is challenging and engaging, often daunting, but can result in changing a disengaged student into a learner.

Figure 3.2: Examples of Transformative Work

Standard	Community Connection	Transformative Work
Seventh-Grade Math Common Core State Standard (RP.A.3): Use proportional relationships to solve multistep ratio and percent problems.	The local community has a large community park with outdoor courts and picnic tables. Many students are excellent soccer players, and soccer seems to be a focus of the local community.	Students conduct a survey on the number of soccer fields per capita in their neighborhood compared to a more affluent neighborhood, analyze the data, and draw conclusions from the information. Students decide on the implications of the findings and present their ideas to city council.
High School History: Students evaluate continuity and change over the course of United States history.	The local neighborhood has a long history. Catholic churches named after Italian saints reflect the neighborhood's earliest immigrants. A famous nightclub from the '30s still contains photos of the famous African American musicians who would play there. Currently, Peruvian and Cuban restaurants dot streets, reflecting the neighborhood's recent immigrants from a variety of Latin American countries.	Students research the history of their changing neighborhood, the reasons and implications of the change, and predict the next iteration in the neighborhood. Then, students identify the key elements of these changes and apply them to changes in U.S. demographics, discussing the complex relationships among change, diversity, and unity.
Third-Grade Common Core State Speaking Standard: Engage effectively in a range of collaborative discussions (one-on-one, in groups, and teacher led) with diverse partners on grade 3 topics and texts, building on others' ideas and expressing their own clearly.	The local community and the classroom community include families from Mexico, Ghana, Indonesia, France, and Russia, as well as Native Americans, African Americans, and European Americans.	All students complete a Cultural Puzzle and share their information with the other members of the class. Then, in small groups, the students discover the commonalities and differences among their classmates and design a plan for creating a caring classroom community.

Strategy 6: Ground the Work in Authenticity

6

The research on work that engages and challenges students stresses authenticity. For decades, Newmann (1992) has argued that engaging school tasks need to connect to the world outside of school and that they must be "meaningful, valuable, significant, and worthy of one's effort" (23). More recently, the National Research Council's (2004) research on engagement also stresses the importance of a real-world connection: the work must have "meaning outside of school." The National Research Council adds that authentic tasks reflect the kind of thinking and challenges that are a part of the discipline: "Ideally, authentic tasks also must be fundamentally linked to problems and modes of reasoning within the subject matter" (66).

This sounds like common sense, for sure. But a look at dioramas in social studies, five-paragraph essays in English classes, and papier-mâché projects in science suggest that some of the work students are asked to do in schools has no counterpart in the world outside of school and is not a part of how those in a discipline think or act. No writer that we've met has put his butt in a chair to write a five-paragraph essay. Instead writers sit down to write essays that explore topics or write commentaries that express their views of the world. Likewise, when Stevi asked her father's science colleagues if any of them created papier-mâché projects, they looked at her as if she were an alien from an unknown planet. Schoolwork that fails to correspond to work that experts in the field do must be reconsidered (Wilhelm 2007). There is no time to waste with inauthentic work.

This concept of authenticity is even more relevant with a glimpse at the Common Core State Standards. In the Standards for Literacy in History/Social Studies, Science, and Technical Subjects, reading and writing are not generic processes. Instead, they are embedded in the discipline itself:

> College and career-ready reading in these fields requires an appreciation of the norms and conventions of each discipline, such as the kinds of evidence used in history and science; an understanding of domain-specific words and phrases; an attention to precise details; and the capacity to evaluate intricate arguments, synthesize complex information, and follow detailed descriptions of events and concepts. In history/social studies, for example, students need to be able to analyze, evaluate, and differentiate primary and secondary sources. When reading scientific and technical texts, students need to be able to gain knowledge from challenging texts that often make extensive use of elaborate diagrams and data to convey information and illustrate concepts. (CCSS 2010, 54)

The basic question we have heard our effective teachers pose is, Is this work that I'm asking students to do worthy of their effort and is it similar to what happens outside of school? If they can't answer yes to both parts of the question, they don't assign the work to the students. Think back to the work John had his seventh graders do. They worked like historians and political advisors, analyzing, interpreting, and making predictions. Just take a look at Jennifer's lesson on probabilities and suspensions. Problem solving is what mathematicians do: they see problems, apply math concepts to the problem, gather data, reach a conclusion, and figure out a way to display their data in a way that is clear to their intended audience. That's what her young mathematicians were doing.

A look at Jennifer's learning targets shows how serious she was that the work reflect the world of mathematicians. Because she wanted to reinforce students' identities as mathematicians, she worded her possible targets accordingly:

- As a mathematician, I can determine the difference between theoretical and experimental probability.
- As a mathematician, I can create tree diagrams based on different situations and calculate the probability of certain events within the situations.
- As a mathematician, I can create Venn diagrams and calculate the probabilities of mutually exclusive events.
- As a mathematician, I can investigate data and draw conclusions that have a direct effect on my life.

Not wanting to leave anything to chance, she named for students how each of those targets mirrored the thinking that mathematicians do.

Linking the Three Strategies of Academic Press, Transformation, and Authenticity

To see what difference these strategies of academic press, transformation, and authenticity make in engaging students in challenging work, we need to return to Jennifer's lesson on probability and suspensions.

"We were looking at proportions and disproportionality, so we split the students into groups based on the population of ethnic groups at our high school. Each student was randomly assigned to one of the groups: black males, black females, Latinas, Latinos, and other. The students received a piece of paper telling them which group they were in. The students took a close look at the numerically dominant groups. Honestly, there was nothing surprising here." The largest population was Latinos, followed closely by Latinas, then black females, then black males. Statistically speaking, "other" was nonexistent. Students were asked to discuss the human data representation with a partner and compare what they saw in the classroom to what they experienced throughout the school.

Next, each student received another card indicating a new group assignment. This new arrangement reflected the number of suspensions for each group. As they reformed their groups something alarming occurred: while Latinos and black females remained proportionally similar, Latinas were cut in half and the grouping of black males doubled. Once again, the students were asked to discuss the findings.

Doing the authentic work of mathematicians, they investigated the data and began drawing conclusions. The volume of student voice increased as the findings became apparent, and black students in the class became visibly upset as they saw the disproportionate number of suspensions for black males. "They knew this was not representative of who they were," Jennifer explained. It is one thing to believe something is wrong; it is quite another to be confronted with the data.

But this was only the beginning. Upon closer investigation the students discovered that black, poor, male students in special education are suspended 67 percent of the time and those same students make up 100 percent of the group of students suspended fourteen or more times. The investigation of data and probability was purposeful and meaningful to all members of the class, even those who were not in the most probable suspension group.

The students then investigated the probability that they personally would be suspended. One student, who often had his head down on the desk and rarely participated in class, proclaimed, "This is fucked up." Language inappropriate, true, but this student was engaged.

Jennifer pumped her fist in excitement. "Another student who sleeps through most of my classes could not wait to get involved in the conversation."

One Latina student inquired, "Doesn't this data affect all of us? I mean, I am applying to college from this high school, and doesn't this data increase the achievement gap?" She was doing what mathematicians do as they work to reach conclusions concerning troubling data.

They were not done yet. Jennifer continued, "The really awesome part was that we went back to the original statistics of our high school, the number of people versus the number of suspensions. I told them to make a choice. Find yourself and your ethnic group, and let's say there were seven students being suspended from your ethnic group. Take yourself out of that mix and see what happens. The students calculated the new percentage based on finding a way to not be a statistic."

The discussion continued. "We talked about institutionalized racism, and the students talked about other places where we see this type of racism happening. It was very close to them."

Rasham was one of the students in Jennifer's class. According to the findings, he would be suspended in the near future. He commented, "It made me realize a lot about the world and how I would like to be one less statistic. I am a lot more determined to prove them wrong about people of color. I will hope that people of color aren't looked down upon one day." The three strategies of academic press, transformation, and authenticity allowed this student, as Freire and Macedo say, "to read the world as well as the word" (1987).

Remember the assistant principal who helped Jennifer plan and teach the lesson, Ms. G? She was in the room the day the students talked about institutionalized racism. After listening to their concerns, she pledged to do something about it. "It was this personal involvement in the work that got my students highly engaged in the learning, and it was the topic that resulted in a social justice focus."

Keep in mind who those students were: more than half were students with special needs, and many of the others were moderately skilled math students. Many of them had a fixed mindset about their ability to do math, and they frequently asked, "What does this have to do with me?" This lesson captured their attention in a way that they will undoubtedly remember. After their work on probability, students could answer those critical questions: Why does this work matter? How will this work help me figure out my place in the world?

Because Jennifer's unit on probability included academic press, transformation, and authenticity, the students were engaged in tough thinking. They were doing work that hooked them and that mattered, and they were definitely in the game.

Reflection

Take a few minutes to think about a future unit in your content area. Complete the following chart as you create work that matters for your students. Consider collaborating with your peers and see what ideas they have to offer.

PLANNING THE NATURE OF THE WORK

Identify the standards and the big ideas of the unit.
Narrow the standards to specific learning targets in student-friendly language.
How would these learning targets look in the world outside of school?
How might this unit matter to students?

List the assets in your local/school community.

How will you include academic press? How will students analyze, interpret data, make predictions, apply their insights, evaluate situations, and create a response?

What might be a problem for them to analyze and solve?

Now put it all together: what major task might you ask students to engage in that has importance and significance?

CHAPTER 4

Work That Matters Daily

Teacher in the Spotlight

 Negar Mizani is a high school English teacher in an urban school in Denver who understands well the challenges of being an immigrant in a new country.

It was 2:00 p.m. in the afternoon, and the temperature in the classroom approached ninety degrees. Thirty-four ninth graders sauntered into their literature class and sat at desks that must have been squeezed into the room with a shoe horn. White, black, Latino, and Latina students sat in prearranged groups sharing jokes, gossip, and a few sarcastic remarks. It was the last period of the day, and the students looked poised for disruption and maybe a little confrontation. Stevi and John looked for a place to sit and were hard-pressed to find one. The windows were open, but the air was still. John wondered aloud how Negar Mizani would pull this off.

Just then Negar counted aloud in a soft voice, "Three, two, one," and the room was silent. These students at Denver East High School, a large urban high school, were ready to think critically, to learn, and, more concretely, to share their ideas in a seminar. They rubbed their foreheads, squinted their eyes, and sat on the desks, the floors, the window sills, as they used critical thinking strategies to wrestle with important work. Negar's students were seeking to unravel the meaning in the assigned readings.

Because of Negar's background, she is ferociously committed to students' thinking at high levels. "I learned English as a second language. I was undocumented until my last year of college, right before my student teaching. I understand struggle. I understand what it's like to be a stranger in a strange country. I understand their reality. My passion to insist on students' critical thinking is driven by my experience. Education saved my life; I would be a statistic without it."

Her passion for her students and her belief in the power of education can be seen everywhere in her classroom. When you arrive in her room, you are taken in by the setting. On one side of the room is a word wall next to examples of outstanding student work. On the other walls are posters of essential questions, intriguing objectives, vocabulary enhancers, and provocative quotes. In the back is an area labeled "think corner." Inviting aesthetically and intellectually, the room reflects the tone that Negar cultivated throughout the year.

Think back to the previous chapter and how Jennifer focused on the nature of the work through higher-order thinking. Negar employed the same principles in her English class. Critical thinking is Negar's way of ensuring that her students analyze and interpret literature, predict what will happen, gain self-knowledge as they apply their insights to their lives, evaluate the authors' perspective, and create their own interpretations of the literature. The vehicle she used regularly to nudge students to do that kind of thinking was the seminar, which led to academic press.

We listened in on one of Negar's classes, absorbed in a discussion of *The Glass Menagerie*. Her directions were brief: listen carefully to each other. After that introduction, the seminar began.

The students began exploring who was the protagonist and who was the antagonist. "I think Tom is the protagonist," one young man hypothesized. "Since the protagonist is a character who learns something, Tom learned the biggest lesson. At the end of the play he did escape, but he was still haunted by the memory of Laura. He realized his mistake and the value of family."

Another boy responded, "I agree. Just the fact that he was the one who told the story proves that he was the protagonist."

"Well," said another girl with a kind and understanding voice, "I thought that Amanda was actually the protagonist. The main part of the story was about her, and she would always be there when Tom would argue. Amanda always wanted to push Laura to whatever she wanted to do. So, it is practically Amanda for the whole play."

"Now that I think about your comments, I think it was Tom," said a girl sitting to the left of the previous speaker. "Because he was the man of the house, or whatever, everything came through him, like all the pressure came to him."

During the majority of the seminar, Negar listened intently, but now she joined the discussion briefly, "What I am hearing is if the story was told from Amanda's perspective, then she would be the protagonist." The students nodded. "So if that's what you think of Amanda, that she is so unreasonable, that would make Tom the villain."

Another student chimed in, "Amanda was more like the antagonist. I think the protagonist is Laura because it always comes back to her. It's Laura and Tom, but it always comes back to Laura at the end."

Negar nudged, "You have to back up your opinion with evidence from the play. Why do you think that?" She then resumed listening and watched them carry on with the seminar.

Anyone visiting the class would have heard multiple perspectives about the play, including what appeared to be a simple question posed by one of the students: who is the protagonist? As an experienced English teacher, Negar could have addressed this question in multiple ways. Students might have completed a worksheet about the literary elements or took notes as she lectured about protagonist and antagonist. However, the answer to the question about protagonist and antagonist is far from a fill-in-the-blank kind of an activity. Since Tennessee Williams wrote the play, experts in the field of literary studies have disagreed about the protagonist of this play, and the discussion continues. Students who wanted to take the easy way out by googling "protagonist in *The Glass Menagerie*" would have found conflicting answers. For instance, SparkNotes claims that Tom is the protagonist while MonkeyNotes asserts that Amanda is in that role, and Schmoop names Tom, Amanda, and Laura all as protagonists. Instead, the students were engaged in the authentic work of literary scholars: using the text to think hard and to form their own interpretations.

How did Negar get her students to do higher-level thinking? How did she get urban students to care about Tom, Amanda, and Laura? What is the nature of Negar's work?

Daily Attention to Authenticity

When book clubs get together, they hash out ideas in the book, exploring themes and questioning the motives of characters. When families sit around the dinner table talking about books they've read, they pose questions and think about the situations in the novels. When literary scholars interpret literature, they wonder about the text, searching for motifs and hunting for the meaning in the text. This is what Negar's students were doing: the authentic work of readers. They weren't filling out worksheets with blanks for naming the protagonist or identifying three symbols in the book. Instead, their ideas and questions moved the conversation forward. This kind of discourse and exploration of ideas is the authentic work that readers need to be doing on a regular basis.

Negar needed her students to understand why she insisted on having them prepare for a Socratic seminar, making sure they understood the reasons for the work. After all, students need to be partners in the learning process and to understand the "how and why" as well as the "what." Black, Dylan, and Harrison (2003), international experts of assessment, stress the importance of teachers' explaining to students what sits behind their teaching: "learning achievements must be made transparent to students to enable them to have a clear overview both of the aims of their work and of what it means to complete it successfully" (52). Students deserve to know the purpose of the work they are doing.

Negar understood that questions such as Why are we doing this? should be celebrated rather than viewed as insubordination. When the teacher explains the research behind her instructional moves, her implicit message is clear: "You are bright, thoughtful students and an integral element in this curriculum. Therefore, I will share the research behind my methods, see what you think and see if you have additional ideas that could make this work even better."

Negar had at her fingertips multiple options for having students reflect with her on the reasons for the instructional tasks in her classroom. One was the reflective journal. When the discussion on point of view and perspective was completed, she asked the students to open their journals and reflect on why she had organized the activity in such a manner. At times, she followed the writing up with a Silent Chalk Talk, where students go to the board and quietly record their ideas for all to see (see Figure 4.1).

Figure 4.1: Silent Chalk Talk

Write a provocative question in the center of a large sheet of chart paper or on a whiteboard. Place markers near the paper or whiteboard. Invite students to stand around the paper or board with the question and explain the rules of a Silent Chalk Talk:

1. No one may talk.
2. Everyone is invited to write his or her thoughts about the question.
3. Everyone is free to respond to the writing of others or to ask a question.
4. Write as many times as you want.
5. Move around the paper to see what others have written.
6. Connect comments with lines or arrows.

At the end of ten to twelve minutes, announce that Silent Chalk Talk is now over. Debrief the experience with them.

Figure 4.2: Other Options for Students Reflecting on the Purpose of the Work

- Share the definition of point of view written by Richard Paul and Linda Elder (2006), leading experts in the field of critical thinking
- Share the research concerning collaboration in the classroom from the National Research Council's book, *Engaging Schools* (2004)
- Hand out a summary of the ideas behind formative assessment using Jan Chappuis' (2009) book *Seven Strategies of Assessment for Learning*
- Show the David Sousa video that presents the brain research on "the person who does the talking does the learning." www.youtube.com/watch?v=UCZxCqUz26E

Other options for helping students understand the reasons for the work include:

- A tutorial focused on debriefing questions such as: Why did I have you define point of view? Why didn't I simply tell you the definition? Why did I have you in pairs for this definition? Why did I time your responses? What is the value of collaboration? Why do we need definitions for concepts?
- Class discussion on an open-ended question connected to the concept under study. For instance, a question to ask might be Why do we discuss perspective if most people keep their perspective no matter what anyone else says or does?
- A problem-solving activity with a short story describing one point of view being presented as the only intelligent view of a subject. In small groups, students discuss this approach to teaching/learning with a synthesis question such as What would you do to address this situation?

In all these cases, the teacher's goal is to spark interest in the reasoning behind the methods for the work, showing that the work is purposeful and intentional. It is to get the students involved in thinking about thinking. This allows the students to understand the importance of having them do the work of a critical thinker. See Figure 4.2 for other reflection options.

Daily Attention to Academic Press

The seminars, the hallmark of Negar's instruction, required students to think critically, a premium skill in the Common Core State Standards and in numerous critiques of secondary education. But what do critical thinkers do? Why is Negar's classroom representative of this behavior?

Critical thinking can be defined as a disciplined way of approaching ideas that involves higher-order thinking. Since the1950s, Bloom's taxonomy has been used to define those higher-order thinking skills. Moving up the ladder of difficulty, the taxonomy began with the lower-order skill of knowledge and progressed to the highest of evaluation. In the 1990s one of Bloom's former students led a group to update the taxonomy so that it reflected twenty-first-century skills. Shifting from nouns to verbs, this updated version reflects the active role of thinking and transposes the importance of evaluation/evaluating and synthesis/creating.

Paul and Elder (2006) define critical thinking this way:

> I think the best way to get to the nub of it is to see that everyone thinks and that their thinking is deeply involved in every dimension of their daily life. If there's one thing that you can't escape, it's your own thinking. It's everywhere you are, and it's always shaping and influencing everything you do—including your emotions and decisions. Every nook and cranny that's in you is thought-ful, i.e., full of thought. The key question is: Are you in charge of your thinking, or is your thinking in charge of you? You discover critical thinking when you realize how deeply the quality of your life is dependent on the quality of your thinking, and that it's possible to take charge of your thinking—to make it what you want it to be rather than what it has been made to be by your environment, your parents, your society, the media, and so on. That's the basic idea behind critical thinking. It's intrinsically connected with a self-determining way of living. It's a commitment to continually upgrade the quality of your thinking so as to upgrade the quality of your life. (454)

Paul's work on critical thinking delves deeper into its nature. He argues that a critical thinker analyzes questions, synthesizes, and critiques ideas. At first glance, Paul's ideas seem to mirror Bloom's original taxonomy, but he goes one step further. The critical thinker reasons out of a cultivated habit. Because of practice, these thinkers regularly dig in to explore assumptions behind all statements and actions, including their own. They scrutinize their own thinking as if they were jewelers studying a shiny rock. Is it a valuable gem or a beautiful but common stone? In fact, some experts of critical thinking deem these traits of metacognition and self-regulation as the most remarkable and, perhaps, the most important (Facione 2011). Through the study of one's own ideas, the student tackles complex issues and investigates the complexity of his or her own thinking.

Arguably, by its very nature, the work undertaken by a critical thinker is often ambiguous, packed with multiple meanings (Strong, Silver, and Perini 2001), and complex, requiring intellectual engagement. Negar's classroom represents "minds-on" pedagogy. She takes her students on a journey examining their own beliefs, the basis of these beliefs, listening and honoring the thoughts of others, and then actively determining their own way of living.

Scaffolding for Academic Press

Negar knew she had to prepare her students for the higher-level thinking required in seminars. Her blueprints for this strategy included a careful design for getting students to this outcome. Consider what Negar did in her unit on perspective: "Today, we are going to discuss perspective and point of view. With your table partner, define these two ideas. Then quickly analyze how they shape the play we just read. Write them down on one of the note cards at your desk. You have three minutes and thirty seconds to complete this task." She turned on the overhead projector so that students could see the timer. "Ready? Go." The timer began counting down.

And how did this prepare students for the seminar? Let's deconstruct what Negar did to build capacity for a seminar as she employed the academic press of critical thinking:

1. Negar activated all student voices in the room. As we know, student voice is vital for a thinking classroom.
2. Negar prepared them for the challenge ahead by allowing students to define and analyze the concept under study: she activated and honored student background knowledge. If a teacher wants students to engage in a challenging, meaningful critical discussion, the students need to practice the skill of doing the thinking in every lesson. The teacher could easily define the concept, but then the teacher would be the primary learner in the classroom.
3. In a small but initially effective way, the teacher created the context for collaboration. The teacher established a basis for a community of learners to work together and move toward the challenging learning goals. Students support each other as they create the answers to the question and rehearse their thinking.
4. The teacher gathered essential formative assessment data. As she checked in with her students, she took notes on where each student stood in relation to the target, in this case, what their understanding of perspective and point of view is, how they expressed themselves, and what questions they were asking. With this information, she would eventually close any gaps in learning.
5. The timer added a sense of urgency. There's no time to waste in this class. When it's time to collaborate and to think together, the students have to get to it.

There was a lot going on in these three minutes and thirty seconds. When the teacher allowed her students to be the focus in defining and analyzing the concepts, necessary ingredients for critical thinking, these preparations took an unmistakable form: setting up students for successful learning.

Scaffolding Through Courage, Humility, and Integrity

As we describe the nature of the work that students are doing, we're talking about more than just the task at hand. It's more than just writing an essay, conducting research, or participating in a seminar. We're also including attention to how students participate in the thinking and in the task itself. The kind of "minds-on" thinkers that we're talking about share a particular set of dispositions or habits of mind. These habits of mind need to be intentionally taught, to be cultivated, and to become an expected part of the work that students do. These qualities take normal discourse into the realm of ethical, critical thinking.

1. **Courage.** Courageous thinkers are willing to voice their thoughts even when their view is a minority opinion. Hand in hand with having the valor to present an unpopular position, they are also courageous in being willing to listen to others. Courage includes the gumption to be right or wrong, to reconsider positions given new facts, and to explore all avenues of thought.
2. **Humility.** Instead of thinking that their opinion is the most important perspective, thinkers with humility are willing to listen to others, realizing that truth can be subjective. They work at listening to understand different perspectives before arguing for theirs. As active listeners, they paraphrase and ask clarifying questions before asserting their perspective.
3. **Integrity.** The disposition of integrity has tremendous ethical implications. Integrity refers to honesty and strong moral principles. All facts are considered, even those facts that challenge the thinker's perspective. Rather than stretching the truth or manipulating facts, a thinker with the disposition of integrity is willing to treat facts with veracity.

Cultivating Courage

Negar knew that for students to be successful critical thinkers in seminars, she needed to nurture those important dispositions, modeling and teaching humility, integrity, and courage. She started this journey in small steps and began preparing them the moment they entered her classroom. From day one, she ensured that all student voices were in the room. Since critical thinking requires student-led discussion, students needed experience explaining and exploring their ideas.

Because participation cannot be an option but a given, Negar didn't rely on those few eager students whose hands would wave in the air when she asked a question. Instead, she regularly asked students to "pair/share" or she randomly called on students, ensuring all students actively participated in the classroom. A firm believer that whoever is doing the talking is doing the learning, she structured her lessons so students were not passively listening but were actively talking, reading, and thinking hard each and every day.

Discussion in Negar's classroom did not resemble the typical classroom. Frequently, classroom discussion follows the I-R-E pattern: the teacher Initiates the question, the student Responds to the teacher's discussion, and the teacher Evaluates the student's response to the teacher's question. And then the pattern continues: initiate, respond, evaluate (Mehan 1979; Wells and Chang-Wells 1992). Instead, Negar cultivated a classroom where students talked to each other and pursued her questions and ones they posed—a simple but important example of authentic work. In the I-R-E patterns, only a few students might talk during the class period, so the quiet, shyer students could get by without being public with their thinking. For many students, it takes courage to talk in class. The I-R-E pattern provides a means for them to hide out.

Negar's classroom mirrors Richard Allington's research on exemplary teachers. Noting that there was scant research on adolescent literacy, Allington (quoted in Beers, Probst, and Rief 2007) set out to learn what happens in those exemplary classrooms that foster substantial growth in literacy, particularly for those students who have struggled in school:

> The focus on developing students' competence with literate conversation sets these classrooms apart from less effective literacy teachers (and science and social studies teachers). The less effective teachers often reported that they just didn't have time for such talk. (281)

Daily Negar created multiple opportunities for all students to talk. The expectation that all would participate prepared students for a seminar where they were the ones doing the exploring, the talking, and the thinking. Remember the girl in the opening seminar who said, "I thought that Amanda was actually the protagonist"? She was a painfully shy member of the class who mustered the courage to respectfully disagree with her classmate. For this young learner, this was courageous.

Of course there is no one way to teach critical thinking. The bottom line here is simple: in order to become critical thinkers, the teacher and the students must practice this skill on a regular basis. Critical thinking challenges everyone to eliminate bias, consider other viewpoints, rethink our own beliefs, and then act on our conclusions. There is nothing easy about this work.

The exemplary classroom is one where students regularly engage in discussion and the instruction shows students how to participate in civil discourse. Reflecting the dispositions so important for a high-quality conversation marked by critical thinking, students know the importance of courage and humility as they considered alterative perspectives. Not only is this an important skill for reading but is also critical for living.

Cultivating Humility

Prior to whole-class discussions, Negar reminded students how to talk and listen to each other as she focused on humility: "Whenever we have a discussion I tell the students, 'I want you to not only listen with your ears, also with your eyes, but most important, with your hearts.'" From the start of the year, she helped students learn how to listen with full attention: "At the beginning of the year we answer the question, What does it mean to listen with your eyes? Your heart? The students tell me what this looks like. I have sentence starters on the board. For example: 'I agree with your point because . . .' 'You made a really good point when you said . . .' 'I hear what you are saying, but . . .'"

Richard Paul and Linda Elder state, "We learn a little and (by nature) think we know a lot. We get limited information and hastily generalize from it. We confuse memorized definitions with deep learning" (2006, 8). Negar's students practice listening "to learn."

Furthermore, Negar nurtured humility as students learned to delay asserting their opinion by waiting until they had listened to others and reconsidered their opinions. Students challenged each other politely and respectfully within a calm atmosphere. Look back at the opening seminar: the atmosphere was thoughtful and welcoming. Comments like, "Now that I think about it . . ." demonstrate the intellectual humility of critical thinkers. Using practices such as talking with a partner, modeling how to disagree with someone's ideas, practicing wait time, and allowing others to participate before you, all contributed to students' ability to honor multiple perspectives.

Regularly students worked in small groups while Negar circulated throughout the room. While eavesdropping, she gauged their effort and nudged them forward. These informal assessments were her opportunities to celebrate students' possibilities even as she refused to accept anything but the best:

- "Okay, love, I really don't know much about this topic, teach me what you know."
- "Yes, I want to disagree with the author here because of my cultural beliefs, but he poses a good argument. I wonder if he is right."

Through her actions and her words, Negar modeled how to be humble.

Nurturing Integrity

Some critical thinkers try to manipulate facts to "win" an argument or to dominate a discussion. A person with integrity seeks the truth. Negar teaches her students to be honest and ethical. Thoughtful questions abound: What evidence do you have to support your idea? How is the author trying to persuade you to think his way? What are the social justice and equity implications of this work?

A young girl summed up the opening seminar discussion, "I think Williams is saying that in reality we need illusion, especially when you have a hard life. Laura had a hard life; she needed her glass animals to distract her so she could have a happy place. For Amanda, the prospect of her daughter getting married and having gentleman callers was her happy place. For Tom, it was going to the movies and being a proprietor or filmmaker. The dilemma is when the illusions are such distractions that they take over your whole life."

This young woman had the integrity to consider all the facts and delve into the author's perspective, which challenged everyone in the room to think about their own illusions and grasp onto reality.

This is the nature of challenging work on a daily basis.

Daily Attention to Transformation

Let's drop in again on *The Glass Menagerie* seminar. Yes, they were critically thinking about the play, but Negar deepened the learning by incorporating the strategy of transformation.

As the seminar continued, Negar guided the discussion to dating someone of a different race or culture and how they would be welcomed (or not) in the home. The students' faces lit up! The students thought hard about how difficult it can be to face reality and how tempting it can be to drift into the world of illusion. One student noted, "I could never bring Enrico home; my dad would have a fit!"

Negar skillfully used the play to activate the students' prior knowledge and provoke self-knowledge as they wrestled with Amanda, Laura, and Tom in this classic drama. The issues they examined in this play mirrored the realities they faced every day, and this transformed the learning to a challenging and engaging event.

Brain scans show that new learning makes sense to students when they are able to connect it to past experiences. As Sousa (2011) points out, substantially more cerebral activity occurs when students connect the new with the familiar, which dramatically improves retention. Negar skillfully guided this connection. Her students understood that she cared about them, that she had high expectations for them, and that she would be there to help them reach challenging goals. Negar knew her students well. She knew their family backgrounds, their avocations, their hopes and dreams. She knew their past successes and failures. She knew her students had funds of knowledge that may not have been tapped until they arrived in her classroom. Vitto in *Relationship Driven Classroom Management* (2003) explains:

> When students work within their areas of affinity and interest, high expectations are naturally set. When we allocate precious instructional time to a

student's strengths and interests, rather than on remediating weaknesses, we send a powerful and affirming message to our students. Teacher expectations are often subtle but always powerful predictors of future outcomes. Teachers who maintain high expectations are able to challenge students to go beyond what they believe they can do. (12)

Negar passionately viewed her students from an asset perspective and refused to view them through the lens of deficits.

From this strength-driven perspective, she built culturally relevant work. We have to remember that culturally relevant does not mean simply bringing in stories written by authors from the same ethnic group or celebrating Kwanzaa and Cinco de Mayo, but it means instead the schoolwork connects directly to the students in the world outside of school. Clearly staying attuned to their lives, Negar regularly used examples from their personal journey, school community, and neighborhoods to clarify complex concepts and build in choices that included student talents and interests.

And this mattered to students. June, one of Negar's students, explained, "When you see that a teacher cares so much, somehow, there's that little, I guess, aroma that ends up coming into the student and the student becomes more interested in what the teacher is teaching and ends up becoming exposed to more challenging and higher level ideas that they wouldn't themselves have thought of."

Students will put effort into the learning when they perceive the work as meaningful. Joan Wink reminds us, "If it is not meaningful to the student, it is not meaningful" (2011, 36). By focusing on student effort and never doubting that with effort they could succeed, Negar reinforced a growth mindset. The messages Negar offered her students are reminiscent of Gary Howard's quote:

An authentic professional relationship is one that communicates clearly to my students through words, my actions, and my attitudes the following sense of connection: "I see you. I acknowledge your presence in this classroom. I know your name and I can pronounce it correctly. I respect your life experiences and your intelligence. I believe in you and I will hold both you and myself accountable to honor your capacity to learn. I enjoy being in this work with you." (2006, 130)

Listen to another of Negar's students, Jacqueline: "Teachers like that, the ones you would go off a cliff for, are the teachers that come in asking you how your day is going, how your other classes are going, how your family is going. They are the ones who invest in you and take the time to get to know you."

Because the seminar in Negar's room touched on what was familiar and, therefore, what was relevant in students' lives, students constructed the meaning of a play written long before they were born. While exploring questions such as who was the protagonist and who was the antagonist, they were guided to think about their lives and began to see how people they knew could be viewed both as an antagonist or protagonist, all depending on the perspective. Literary elements, then, took on a meaning grander than just being able to identify them in a piece of literature. Negar skillfully ensured that her students' lives were an integral part of the curriculum; this is transformative teaching.

One of her students described it this way: "There is a difference between teaching 'these are my ideas, they are my thoughts, this is what you should believe, blah, blah, blah.' Ms. Mizani did a good job of not having to steer students, like, oh, this is what you should do or this is what you should think. Because of how she set up the classroom, students would think like, hey, wait, that makes sense, and then they end up building off of that and create something totally new from it."

Clock Watchers and the Delicious Classroom

In *Clock Watchers* (2009) we shared our insights into how teachers can create the context that is likely to motivate and engage students in their learning. Negar brought those six Cs into reality, resulting in exciting classes where students were challenged daily and wanted to continue learning. In Negar's classroom, students continued to build the caring classroom through working collaboratively in a respectful environment. They were challenged as they investigated their thinking on an issue or a question relevant to their lives. As they collaborated, they learned to listen to and learn from different points of view. They had choice in their resources and data gathering and the focus of their discussions. Negar consistently checked in with the groups, offering supportive and specific comments designed to scaffold learning. Finally, the seminar was a celebration of student thinking and learning. The six Cs came together to support students as they met the challenge of critical thinking.

Teaching is challenging, frustrating, and often overwhelming for teachers who care deeply about their craft. Is Negar successful every day with every class? Of course not. However, how she responded to the challenges speaks volumes to why her students love her and perform for her. June described it this way, "I had a class this year where I know for a fact if I would have had someone like Ms. Mizani or countless other excellent teachers, the class would have been amazing. Seriously her class was delicious!"

Teachers who believe in their students' ability to do challenging work take responsibility for student learning. As Negar explained, "When class doesn't work, it's rarely the fault of the children. Like in my seventh-period class today. I'll be honest, it was not as organized as I wanted it to be; obviously, the last ten minutes of the lesson did not work. So I needed to revamp this part of the lesson. As a result, my eighth-period class had a more meaningful ending. I feel like I am constantly reflecting on my practice. It wasn't the fault of the students; I was the issue. I didn't think of the right way or the right approach, and I have to reflect on what I could do better and implement it."

As Negar concluded, "Sometimes we fail to realize the wealth of knowledge our students bring to class with them. I am here to learn from them as much as they are here to learn from me. I think making sure that students are given opportunities to rely on each other's expertise to solve problems is essential. This is challenging work."

This is delicious.

Window into Practice: After

As you read the following vignette describing Mr. Lynne a few months after the vignette that opened Part 2, consider the differences in the work that students are doing. Where is there evidence of academic press, transformation, or authenticity? What difference does this work make in student engagement?

Just as the bell finished ringing, a few students raced to their seats. "Glad you made it, Hector. We're just about to figure out what we can do about the concern you raised yesterday."

Mr. Lynne turned to the class, "How many of you live close by the school?" Nearly everyone raised their hands. "And how many of you have heard your family talk about what Hector told us about yesterday, those proposed high-rises over on Lowell Boulevard?" Again, nearly everyone's hands went up.

"It's not fair, mister." Jose, usually quiet and withdrawn, blurted out. "Those rich, white folks are going to kick us out of our homes."

Other students chimed in. "My grandmother's lived in that house nearly all her life, and now they want to tear it down and build those apartments."

"They don't care about us."

Mr. Lynne signaled for them to quiet down. "Remember, we've been talking about how every issue has multiple viewpoints. We don't have to agree with them, but we do need to recognize them. So let's just brainstorm who might have a stake in the high-rise issue."

As the students began their list, Mr. Lynne pushed them. "And what would your neigh-bor's perspective be? What's another perspective? And what would that person say?" When the conversation became too animated, he reminded them. "I didn't say you had to agree with them, just that you had to recognize those different perspectives."

As the list on the board grew, he paused the conversation. "We've talked about the power of writing all year. Now we're going to experience it firsthand. Here's your task. You're going to be like Gary Soto and Sandra Cisneros and explore these conflicts through writing short stories. This is going to be tough, I'm warning you, because you're going to write from lots of different perspectives. On top of that, we're going to select a couple to send the *North Denver Tribune*." He held up a copy of the local newspaper. "I told you that one of the editors is very interested in what you have to say. She's even willing to print a few of your stories."

He continued explaining the assignment. "For your first story, you'll work with a partner and select a couple of different perspectives from our list. Then remember that plot diagram we've used throughout the year? I want that to guide you as you plan your story. Your job is to show me how you understand how that diagram shapes a story and how fiction can make a difference. Are you ready to begin?"

PART 3

Student Access

Window into Practice: Before

As you read this vignette, consider what Ms. Johnson's actions suggest about her beliefs and assumptions around students and learning. What does she think about providing all students access to challenging learning? At the end of Part 3, you'll return to her classroom to see what changes occurred after reflecting on access.

Ms. Johnson met her students with a smile and welcomed them into the class. "OK, today we are going to show what we learned about the Middle East. You know the drill: you are to write a five-paragraph essay demonstrating your understanding of the events in this part of the world from 1948 through today."

The students were told the day before this essay exam that they needed a thesis statement, support, and a conclusion following the format of the traditional five-paragraph essay. Ms. Johnson was sure this challenging assessment would show who had been doing their homework, listening in class, and being the learner she wanted all of her students to be.

"Ms. Johnson, could I leave the room?" asked Ahmad, a very personable young man with low writing skills.

Ms. Johnson walked to the back of the room and quietly informed Ahmad, "You do this all the time. I know you are capable of this work. Stay here and give it a try."

"Why?" Ahmad remarked. "I never get anything above a D on these kinds of tests."

"You just need to work harder."

"Yeah, right." Ahmad sat staring at the paper and not writing a word.

Ms. Johnson moved around the silent room to check in on other students. She noticed Frank.

"What are you doing on your paper, Frank?"

"I am doodling in the margins."

"You need to get rid of that paper and start all over again, hurry up, or you'll run out of time!"

"Why? These drawings help me organize my thoughts."

"This is a formal assignment; do you think your employer is going to want work with drawings on it?"

Just then, Marissa asked, "Why do we always have to write? I hate writing."

Ms. Johnson had had enough. "Look, this is the real world. You have to write in order to survive in this global economy. No one is going to hold your hand out there! If you choose not to do this essay, then live with the consequences."

Later that night, she was assessing students' progress. As she plodded through the other essays, she became distraught. "What is wrong with these kids? They don't want to work. They just don't care."

> The greater danger for most of us lies not in setting our aim too high and falling short, but in setting our aim too low and achieving our mark. —**Michelangelo**

CHAPTER 5

Opening Up Access to the Tough Work

Teachers in the Spotlight

Lesli Cochran is the middle school humanities teacher whose classroom we've visited throughout this book.

Alisa Wills-Keely is the high school teacher whose classroom we've watched several times.

Kathy Cocetti is a high school English teacher in the Denver suburbs.

Steve Lash is Kathy's teaching partner, who teaches both English and social studies.

Martha Tudor is a high school science teacher in a small community in Kentucky.

A Critical Incident: An Entry from Stevi's Blog

Not too long ago, Stevi wrote on her blog about a critical incident in her teaching, an incident she had reflected on over the years:

> Sometimes all it takes is one comment to rock our world. One innocent comment and our world shifts around us. Like you could guess, that comment occurred on a day like any other day at the high school where I taught. As

usual at lunch time, teachers sauntered into the English department office either with a tray from the cafeteria or with their packed lunch. I must have beat everyone in because I remember shaking off thoughts of my last class, Practical English, a class that I loved to teach but one that other teachers shied away from. Louis had told the story of his father getting into trouble with the law one more time, and Joe complained about having to close late at work the night before. That class, mostly boys, was sometimes tricky to settle down, but once we got into a groove, they often surprised me. Right now we were in the middle of a mock business venture where they had to determine the qualities of a person they'd hire, then develop interview questions and design the application form. It was a task they enjoyed and that had prompted some hot and heavy conversation.

Just as I was thinking about Louis' comment about whether or not a criminal record should matter in hiring decisions, our department chair walked into the office. Often her stories of her AP class were entertaining and stories that greatly differed from those I might tell about Practical English.

"You know," she began, "I looked around the room today and noticed that I have a lot of girls in AP, and they sure are blond!" She sat down and began eating her salad.

And I pictured my Practical English class: those boys sure were not blond. Louis' last name was Lucero, and Joe's last name was Italian, can't remember all these years later, but I do know that I had a Gonzales and a Gomez in class. And one of the few African American students in our school sat in the third row.

Blond, huh?

And my guys weren't.

Her girls were learning about Hawthorne and Hemingway. My guys were learning about business writing and filling out forms. Her girls were writing extended essays while my guys were writing letters of complaint. Her girls were talking about going to college and my guys were worrying about jobs.

And hers were blond and mine weren't.

Yep, one comment that day at lunch shifted my world and knocked me awake (http://stevi-steviq.blogspot.com/).

The Need to Focus on Student Access

Until that moment Stevi hadn't thought about how our education system limited access to certain content for certain students, and all too often the students who were not part of the "literacy club" (Smith 1987) were poor and dark and often male. As well-meaning as the English teachers were, they hadn't figured out ways that they could provide entry points for all students to wrestle with challenging curriculum. As Stevi thought back to that time, she realized that they just accepted the prevailing thought of the time that only those who were ready and headed to college could read complex text. Because she adored her Practical English kids, she worried about burdening them with difficult text that was divorced from their day-to-day lived experience. However, what she realized that day in the English office was that she had limited them by not even entertaining the thought of challenging them, of not making sure they had access to the tough intellectual work too often reserved for those girls who "sure were blond."

Remember Lesli's students in Chapters 2 and 3? The students sitting in Lesli's eighth-grade class were a special group indeed. Every single one of them had some kind of a label, and a look at the class roster would suggest that Lesli was teaching a special ed class or a class for troubled kids. Her eighth graders were similar to Stevi's students in Practical English. What Stevi could have learned from her!

From the first day Lesli met them, she thought about them as high school students. Traditionally, the first unit of the year in the nearby high school was *Romeo and Juliet*.

Conversation About Student Access and CCSS

John: Did you notice the emphasis on collaboration in Common Core? Students are expected to engage in "collegial discussions" where they present ideas and build effective arguments. What I like about that standard is that it supports what we know about how well-designed group work is a means for accessing challenging content.

Stevi: Interesting that that collaboration is both a goal and a scaffold. So many of the schools where I work are figuring out ways to support students new to English, and collaboration is certainly important for students to become proficient in a new language.

John: Right! Talk is vital for learning for all students including students learning English. That's when they get to practice using academic language as they debate the causes of the Civil War or examine the results of a scientific experiment.

Stevi: I wonder why Common Core includes speaking only in the standards for English language arts? In each grade students are expected to participate "in a range of collaborative discussions" where they present and defend their claims. Speaking as a scientist or as an historian is as important as reading and writing like one. After all, we build arguments and present information in all content areas, but speaking appears explicitly only in English language arts.

John: Just because it's not there doesn't mean it shouldn't be there.

Stevi: That's particularly true if we really want all students to access challenging content. They have to work collaboratively, and talk plays a pivotal role in growing our understanding.

Lesli worried that some of the high school teachers used this unit as a way of sorting kids: those who could handle Shakespeare were ready for the college track while those who couldn't would land in general ed or remedial courses. She wanted to make sure that her eighth graders had enough background knowledge and cognitive strategies to access the content and to be successful high schoolers. Near the end of the year, she set out to teach them a Shakespearean play in order to build their background knowledge, refine the thinking strategies they had been working on all year, and develop even more ways for them to navigate difficult text at an independent level.

"I had to hook them first," she explained. "One of the problems my team and I had been addressing was their language. They had the worst potty mouths of any students I've ever taught. So I used that as an entry point. We talked about cursing, Shakespearean style." Hooking them meant viewing their problematic use of language as a place to begin. So she set about teaching them the slang of the time and Shakespeare's unique ways of expressing disdain. Occasionally she would place quotes on the board and ask students to pair up to translate the quote into contemporary language. One quote was: "Curse your throat, you bawling dog." Jerardo didn't wait to talk it over with his partner. Instead, he spontaneously hollered out, "I get it! It means 'shut up, you bitch.'" Then realizing his use of inappropriate language, he blushed and mumbled, "Sorry, Miss."

On the final, Lesli asked students to explain strategies that they would use to make meaning of a new Shakespearean play when they hit high school. The students listed coding the text, making connections, and talking to a classmate when confused. When Lesli overheard one of her students at lunch, she knew that her students were no longer intimidated by Shakespeare. Her student, arms crossed and eyebrows scrunched together in anger, hurtled a curse unlike any other: "You're just a frothy tickle-brained popinjay!" She had further proof that this group of heavily labeled students was no more encumbered by those labels during an end-of-year, schoolwide activity. All the school's eighth graders could pick from a choice of various activities. Many of Lesli's students selected to play a quiz game in order to compete against other classes. Their favorite category was Shakespeare, and they rocked as they answered question after question.

Now is a critical time for teachers to think about access for all students to challenging, complex work. The Common Core State Standards are explicit that these standards apply to all students, not just a privileged group. In Lucy Calkins' book *Pathways to the Common Core* (2012), she argues:

> The CCSS emphasize that every student needs to be given access to this work. Students with IEPs (individualized education programs) still need to be taught to question an author's bias, to argue for a claim, to synthesize information across texts. Teachers are invited to use assisted technology or other scaffolds to be sure that every learner has access to the thinking curriculum that is at the heart of the CCSS. (12)

Even before the CCSS, Lesli, like the other teachers we had studied, knew how to provide access to challenging intellectual work. As we studied them, we noted three strategies they all used for granting access to demanding content: a caring classroom community, checking in to move forward, and autonomy through choice.

If only such strategies had propped up Stevi's practice those years ago, she might have done a better job for the boys in Practical English.

Strategy 7: Create a Caring Classroom Community of Learners

The word *community* has its roots in the Latin word *communitas*—*cum* translating to "with" or "together" and *munus* meaning "gift." So within the word *community* is a reminder of the gift that we give each other when we collaborate in fellowship. At a school where Stevi worked in her early days of teaching, the school's motto was "Our links make us strong." And in a classroom community, the quality of the social network that links all the individuals in the group together matters.

Lesli's students understood the power of community. Listen to what they had to say in an interview about their class that year:

"When we were first in Mrs. Cochran's classroom, we had too many different types of people in there. We worried about getting people to like and accept you."

"Yeah, it was challenging to fit it, and to tell you the truth, I was scared."

"We had so many different types of people and we wondered if we would get along."

Figure 5.1: Peck's Stages of Community

Scott Peck's Process of Community Building
(from *The Different Drum: Community-Making and Peace*)

1. **Pseudo community:** Early in the process of becoming a community, people present their best sides and aim to be nice. Conflict is often avoided so the group appears polite and congenial.
2. **Chaos:** Over time people in the group begin to show their not-so-nice selves and conflict emerges. In other community-building models, this is referred to as "norming and storming."
3. **Emptiness:** Moving beyond attempts to fix the chaos, the group recognizes that certain assumptions don't serve them well, so they begin to empty themselves of defense mechanisms and allow themselves to be vulnerable.
4. **True community:** Now the group can become an authentic community which is defined as deep respect, listening, and compassion. (1998)

"She always made us work in partners even with people we didn't know, and she made sure we knew each other's names. At first I worried about who was going to be my partner. But now we can be partners with anyone."

When asked what had made the difference, several students laughed. "No one makes fun of anyone else: Ms. Cochran would stop us if we did."

"People who are different are not bullied; we trust each other."

"Now we know each other, and we can open up with each other. She made us feel safe and we learned that we could trust each other."

For this group of eighth graders, that sense of safety was critical. As one student explained, "When we had to give a speech at the end of the year, we were scared. It was hard to do, but we had courage because we knew each other."

"She forces us to do things that took us out of our comfort zone, and if we didn't trust each other, I don't think we would have done it."

Community and Risk Taking

This awareness of working out of the comfort zone was important. Students have to have moments—and many of them—of discomfort. In the world of Critical Friends Groups (CFGs), a type of professional learning community where educators get together voluntarily to improve their practice through collaborative learning, we talk about the zones of comfort, risk, and danger. The comfort zone is where we work when we know what to expect and we're confident about our skills to be successful. The danger zone is just the opposite: the task at hand petrifies us and we shut down. However, the middle zone, the area where we take risks, is that edgy place where we learn and stretch (see Figure 5.2).

Figure 5.2: Zones of Comfort, Risk, and Danger

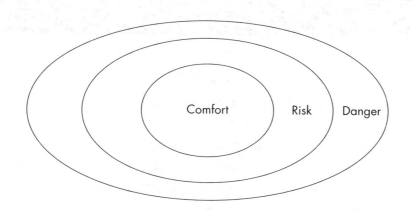

Those three zones describe Stevi as a skier. Often she would start by skiing the green-coded easy slopes because they were in her comfort zone. She could warm up and get her ski legs back on these gentle slopes. Most of the day, though, she had the most fun skiing the blue-coded slopes with their steeper terrain and tricky bumps. When she skied with friends who were stronger skiers than she, she was urged to ski slightly more difficult slopes. Unfortunately, now and then she'd find herself on a slope that was way too difficult—those black-coded slopes. That's where she skied in her danger zone, and it wasn't a pretty picture. On those slopes most of her techniques and skills disappeared. She would freeze and was known to take off her skis and hobble down the hill. It wasn't fun, and all she learned was that she wasn't a good skier and that she never wanted to face that run again.

For Lesli's students to work in the risk zone, they needed that community. In the past, this group of students had prided themselves on being tough and the opposite of school nerds. Many had worked hard at building an anti-"school boy" (or girl) persona, so reading Shakespeare was crossing into a foreign land without a passport. To let their guard down, they had to be in a community of support where they knew they mattered to each other and where the norm was to be respectful and supportive. Students can work in that risk zone only when they are in a caring classroom community (see Figure 5.3).

This is a lesson for all learners, regardless of age. Recently John was co-teaching a class of seventy-five college students who were crammed into a double-wide campus trailer with huge posts in the middle of the classroom and fans blowing loudly. The facility was horrendous, and his students were dissatisfied to say the least. When John and his co-instructors gathered exit cards from the students, one message resonated, "I don't feel like anyone knows me in this large group; I do not feel a part of a

Figure 5.3: Emotional Safety

Emotional Safety
Sense of belonging
Clear understanding of expectations
Predictability of consequences
Freedom from harassment
Freedom to make choices
Freedom from prejudice
Freedom of expression (Vitto 2003, 46)

Figure 5.4: CCSS Call for the Social Nature of Learning: Speaking and Listening

Including but not limited to skills necessary for formal presentations, the Speaking and Listening standards require students to develop a range of broadly useful oral communication and interpersonal skills. *Students must learn to work together, express and listen carefully to ideas*, integrate information from oral, visual, quantitative, and media sources, evaluate what they hear, use media and visual displays strategically to help achieve communicative purposes, and adapt speech to context and task. (Common Core State Standards 2010, 8) (italics added)

community." John and his cohorts worked diligently to solve the problem. The message was clear: if adult learners feel a lack of safety in a classroom, imagine the effect on young learners.

Collaboration: Vygotsky and the Social Nature of Learning

Not only do students attest to the importance of community, but so does Lev Vygotsky's research (Tharp and Gallimore 1988). Coining the term *zone of proximal development* (also called "zone of actual development"), Vygotsky described the learning zone as ranging from what learners cannot do alone to what they can do over time with social support and finally to what they can do on their own (see Figure 5.5).

Think about driving a car. When we first learn to drive, we're early in the zone where we need someone sitting next to us, talking us through all the decisions we need to make. Often parents take us to an empty but large parking lot for practice. At that point, driving is something we can't (or shouldn't) do alone. (Stevi learned this lesson the hard way. Before she had her driver's license, she "borrowed" the family car and had two minor accidents in the space of twenty minutes.) Throughout the journey of learning to drive, we have time to practice, nearly always under the wing of a

Figure 5.5: Zone of Proximal Development

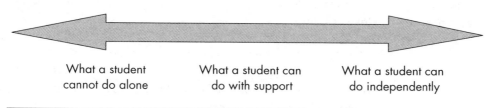

| What a student cannot do alone | What a student can do with support | What a student can do independently |

more "capable other" who offers us guidance and feedback. Eventually, we move along the zone to the point where we can drive alone. The voice of our parents or of our driver's ed teacher whispers (and sometimes shouts) in our ear. "Don't forget to adjust the mirror. Follow a car length's distance for every ten miles of speed. Slow down. The yellow light is going turn red before you get there." Eventually their inner voice becomes integrated into ours. Vygotsky's research suggests that students can actually do more difficult work when they are working collaboratively. During that process and through interacting with others, they learn both what to think and how to think (Frey, Fisher, and Everlove 2009).

Strategy 8: Check in to Move Forward

Not too long ago, Stevi joined a high school staff for its annual faculty retreat. The large staff was divided into groups of four or five and assigned various tasks. The first task required orienteering skills. After the team leader briefly explained how to read a compass and how to navigate with nothing other than a topographical map and a compass, Stevi's group was sent off to find an unknown object at a specific location in the woods. After about an hour, they knew that they were close but struggled to find the object, despite their confidence that their calculations were correct. Finally they found what they were looking for, about sixty feet away from where they had figured.

The team leader checked in with Stevi's group after their initial failure in finding the object. Through questioning, the team leader helped the group reflect on what worked well and where they went amiss. What the group had failed to do was to clarify where they were on the topo map when they first started. Their calculations put them close to the starting point but were not exact. With that brief check-in and that one bit of feedback, Stevi's group set off again with a new object to find. This time they were successful: not sixty feet off, not ten feet off, but right on target.

Productive Failure

What Stevi and her group encountered was "productive failure," failure that leads to success. By working collaboratively, checking in with their team leader, and reflecting on their actions, they were able to readjust their thinking, sharpen their skills, and achieve success. Frey, Fisher, and Everlove's (2009) research corroborates Stevi's experience with productive failure:

> It seems that when the task is structured so that it is difficult, but not impossible, learners actually outperform those who were in groups that had tasks that ensured success. Groups truly need a problem that might result in an incorrect answer, a failed experiment, or inaccurate conclusion. (21)

It may sound odd to say that failure of any sort is a way of providing access to challenging work. However, failure, when couched in a caring community and accompanied by self-assessment (which we called checking in and checking out in *Clock Watchers* [2009]) along with feedback, can be powerful.

We can pull lessons from successful people who failed time and time again but eventually were successful:

- Henry Ford's early business ventures were failures. In fact, he went broke five times before he founded his successful automobile company.
- Colonel Sanders' famous recipe for Kentucky Fried Chicken was rejected 1,009 times before a restaurant finally accepted it.
- Albert Einstein was booted out of school and considered intellectually slow since he didn't speak until he was four and didn't read until he was seven.
- Winston Churchill failed sixth grade and didn't win even one election until he was sixty-two, when he became prime minister of England. (www.onlinecollege .org/2010/02/16/50-famously-successful-people-who-failed-at-first/)

It seems that failure might play a vital role in a successful life. In fact, Hattie (2012b) asserts that error leads to opportunities to grow:

> error should not be considered the privilege of lower-achieving students. All students (as all teachers) do not always succeed the first time, nor do they always know what to do next, and nor do they always attain perfection. This is not a deficit, or deficit thinking, or concentrating on the negative; rather it is the opposite in that acknowledging errors allows for opportunities. . . . Knowing this error is fundamental to moving towards success. (115)

Perhaps it's time that we start celebrating failures and acknowledging how risk means possible failure. And, of course, it's about the support that teachers offer along the way. It's about an attitude that says, "Maybe you can't do it right now, but you will."

The Power of Yet

In the tenth century, Bishop Joseph Hall declared that "perfection is the child of time." Recently at a conference, we heard Carol Dweck echo Bishop Hall's sentiment. As she explained her research on mindset, she stated, "When people say they can't do something, they need to add the word 'yet.' So when you think about not being able to play the piano, say it like this: I can't play the piano . . . yet. Or I can't do quadratic equations . . . yet" (2012). As John and Stevi were working on this book, they adopted Dweck's perspective. In more than one email, one of them would write something like: "I can't get the words right in this part . . . yet."

This belief in the power of yet can be seen in classrooms where students are engaged in work that was toward the far end of their zone of proximal development. The teachers we've studied know that their job—and their challenge—is to put into action the force of that one simple word: *yet*. If they seriously want students to access challenging content, they have to be clear about their learning targets, provide the scaffolding that will lead students to meet those targets, invite students to self-assess, and have a system in place for both the students and the teacher to track that growth. Furthermore, it's important for those teachers to provide multiple opportunities for students to reach their targets.

Getting to Yet at the Start of the Year

Alisa Wills-Keely is a master of this strategy. She knows the work she assigns students is challenging, and she knows that students will have to exert an effort over time to meet her expectations. One of the many ways she ensures that all students have access to knowledge and skills is by making sure they have a substantial amount of time to work in class. "Sure, I could talk at them all the time, but that won't accomplish a thing. For them to succeed, they have to actually do the work, not listen to me talk about it. And that requires time."

Often at the start of the school year, students don't *yet* have the stamina to stay focused for an extended period of time, so she sets out to build that stamina. Early in the year, she tends to do much of the guiding, moving slowly as she teaches students how to work in a group, how to annotate text, how to self-assess, and how to be ready for a conference. Her slow pace is intentional and carefully crafted. "Even though I'm sick of my voice," she commented, "I know that to hear their voices engaged in learning, I have to build their stamina. I have to model, coach, confer, and teach. That's how I can move both those who struggle academically and those who rarely struggle enough."

Organizing her class time as a workshop she begins with a minilesson in which she models for students the kind of thinking that she wants them to do. Since one of her goals is for students to be able to have extended discussion about meaty topics, she must teach them what a good discussion entails. As discussed in Chapter 2, she often provides protocols to guide the discussion, but at the start of the year and even with the protocol, students end their discussions too early and don't push each other's thinking nearly enough to go deep into their learning.

To build their stamina for in-depth discussions, she might model how to pose questions that move the discussion forward, how to disagree respectfully, or how to cite the text to justify an opinion. During work time, while students explore a text or an issue, she carefully monitors their discussions. When necessary, she catches their attention, following Bennett's (2007) description of the workshop model. Bennett uses a fly-fishing metaphor of catch and release to reflect the importance of students' being active in the learning process:

> During the work time, student stamina for work may wane, and it is time for another "catch" from the fisherman. So we pull students out of the river of learning and give them another round of teacher talk—to show students *how* and remind them *why* the task we are asking them do is important. But, and this is a big but—ONLY FOR A FEW MINUTES! It is crucial to throw them back in to reading, writing, and talking *before they stop breathing*. Students need lots of time to swim in texts and talk in order to learn. If teachers are doing all of the talking, they are the ones swimming—and doing all the work. (10)

Alisa explained, "I move around the room watching and listening. Then I catch their attention after a few minutes to give them another pointer." Sometimes that pointer is a celebration of the kind of discourse that she's hearing and sometimes it's a specific lesson on paraphrasing or redirecting a discussion in an invitational manner. "I'll catch them the first few days after about five minutes since often that's when I hear a lull in the conversation. Then each day I wait a few more minutes before I catch them. Next week, for instance, I should be able to let them discuss for twenty-five minutes without any guidance from me. At that point I'll want to highlight with them what's going well and what they've figured out about working together. It's all about building stamina."

Getting to Yet Through Self-Assessment

John has struggled with his golf game for years. Early on in his amateur career, John thought his swing was fine. But as he read more and watched others who were far better players than he was, he wanted to improve. But all of his reading and watching expert videos did not help; he remained average at best. He had nearly given up hope when he visited a local indoor golf academy that had cameras set up to record his swing from the side view and the back view. These cameras gave instant feedback on the not-so-wonderful elements of John's swing. Most important, after a very few minutes of actual instruction, John could manipulate the video to focus in on key mistakes he was making. John, on his own, could draw lines on the video screen to track the movement of his club and his body. John was assessing his own golf swing and could make improvements on the spot. Nothing had the impact of improving John's golf game like his ability to assess his own progress and see his swing improve before his eyes. For the first time, John understood the key elements of a good golf swing.

In *How the Brain Learns* (2011), Dr. David Sousa offers insight into why student involvement in the assessment process is more likely to result in successful learning. Dr. Sousa focuses on retention:

> The assignment of sense and meaning to new learning can occur only if the learner has adequate time to process and reprocess it. This continuing reprocessing of information is called rehearsal and it is a critical component in the transference of information from working memory to long-term storage. . . . Time is a critical component of rehearsal. Initial rehearsal occurs when the information first enters working memory. If the learner cannot attach sense or meaning, and if there is not time for further processing, then the new information is likely to be lost. . . . Allowing the learner to go beyond the initial processing . . . allows the learner to review the information, to make sense of it, to elaborate on the details, and to assign value and relevance, thus increasing significantly the chance of long-term storage. (86)

As John improved his understanding of the golf swing, he had to invest the time to practice his newfound understandings. Likewise, convinced that students must be an integral part of the assessment process, Alisa makes sure that students have time to make meaning of new learning, understand the learning targets, and reflect on their progress toward the targets. She adds: "If students can't tell you how close they are to the learning target, then either I haven't been clear enough or I haven't modeled enough for them."

In the past, Alisa had students complete self-assessments in which they indicated if they were approaching, meeting, or exceeding the learning targets. However, she noted that some students were similar to John when he was first learning the game of golf. Remember how he initially thought his swing was fine until his understanding about effective swings grew deeper? The students, too, rated themselves higher early in a unit than they did as the unit progressed. Through conferring with students, Alisa learned that they lowered their rating as they gained more practice and information, realizing how naïve their initial understanding was. Because of this insight, she revised the form so that students could reflect on their understanding, providing evidence and an explanation of their thinking (see Figure 5.6).

Another shift in thinking that illustrates the "power of yet" is Alisa's awareness that students needed multiple opportunities to write in a variety of genres, read different kinds of texts, and engage in meaningful discourse. With the advent of the Common Core State Standards she was even more convinced that the standards needed to spiral throughout the year. "After all, who is going to be proficient at the standard about writing arguments and using valid reasoning after one or two experiences? This has to

Figure 5.6: Alisa's Revised Self-Assessment Form

Learning Target	Explanation	Approaching	Meeting	Exceeding
I can . . .				
I can . . .				
I can . . .				

happen over and over. I need to make sure that students have multiple opportunities to do this kind of intellectual work."

No longer believing that students could master the standards at the end of one unit or one quarter, it became clear to her that access to demanding intellectual knowledge meant that some learning targets must advance to higher levels throughout the year. True, students may demonstrate proficiency on an assignment, but this kind of intellectual engagement needs rehearsal, practice, and more practice, and, as students gain confidence and skill in difficult work, they need different levels of support.

Checking in Through Conferring

Because conferring is an integral part of her practice to ensure all students can access challenging content, Alisa warned everyone early in the year that she would be hovering over them while they're working. "I warn them that I'm the creepy teacher. They need to know that. There is no boundary between their space and mine. That boundary simply doesn't exist. I know I'm creepy when I cross it, and I'll take that criticism. I warn them that when they're working I won't be at my computer reading my email or balancing my checkbook. I'll be right next to them, invading their body space. If I don't lean in and read what they're writing, if I don't sit down beside them and listen hard to their conversation, and if I don't watch them annotate, how am I going to support them to grow? How will I know what they need at this moment in time?"

In the past, her typical conferences centered on group work. Spending time with each group, she was able to learn how they collaborated and how the thinking of the group was growing. With clipboard in hand, she kept brief notes about what she learned about the group and what her teaching points were. Daily, she "touched base" with every student in class but wasn't focused on learning about each individually as long as the group seemed to be headed in the right direction.

However, as she reflected on the results of those conferences, she was dissatisfied. "I'm good at conferring with groups and seeing how the group is progressing. Often my conferences were short and focused, but what I figured out was that I was missing out on learning what each student could do independently." She is still haunted by the "one that got away." A former student, a bright boy, refused to work for her. As she pondered what happened, she realized that she hadn't spent enough time getting to know him and building that important relationship. Even though the student had gone on to other teachers, Alisa continued thinking about him and eventually realized that he had given her a gift. Because of her failure to reach him, she was pressed to reflect on a part of her practice that wasn't up to her standards and to figure out what she needed to shift so that no student would sit in her class refusing to learn.

To remedy that dissatisfaction, Alisa decided she needed to confer less often with groups so she would have time daily for individual conferences. She gave herself permission to linger longer with each student. "I want to relax in my conferences so I can soak in their thinking for a bit. I want them to tell me a story and not just gloss over their learning. In the past, I haven't dug deep enough. I don't have to confer with everyone every day, but I do need to spend quality time with each student every couple of weeks. I have to dig more into their thinking to understand what they know and where their sticking points are. The only way to do that is to sit beside them and listen to them think and work."

In her conferring, she has become much more intentional about probing students about the learning targets and urging them to show her how they are working with them. In other words, it's not enough for students to give her a nod and say that they've met them. They need to show her their thinking and how they're working toward those goals.

Through her conferences with both groups and individuals, Alisa is able to determine whether all her students, those who have historically done poorly in school and those who have met the standards, have access to the content and knowledge and are continuing to grow. That frequent and very personal checking in allows her to determine next steps and figure out if students need more scaffolding or if it's time to remove the scaffolding that she's providing.

Feedback That Moves Students Forward

With frequent checking in, Alisa is able to provide feedback that has the potential to move students from where they are to where they need to be. One of the top-ten influences on achievement, feedback—when done well—can have tremendous power. However, not all feedback is effective. Educational researcher John Hattie points out: "while feedback is among the most powerful moderators of learning its effects are among the most variable" (2012b, 115). Feedback that matters narrows the distance between where students are and where they need to be. For feedback to reach its potential, Hattie notes that feedback works best at three levels:

- **Task:** Corrective and specific feedback focused on the product, the work itself. This is when Alisa focuses on the essay that students are writing and shows them spots where she's confused as a reader or points out errors in conventions.
- **Process:** Guidance about how to complete the task with an emphasis on how the work is done. When Alisa shows students how she draws inferences to make meaning, she is providing the feedback that will help them know *how* to tackle difficult text. In conferences when she models her writing process, she is showing them the thinking process of a writer.
- **Self-regulation:** Feedback focused on metacognition with students monitoring their own progress and self-assessing regularly. Alisa's focus on self-regulation can be seen when she poses questions about whether or not they understood difficult text or when she urges them to think about times when they successfully tackled a difficult problem and name their thinking process. Her self-assessment forms also promote self-regulation.

Hattie names a fourth level of feedback, self, and then offers a serious warning. Under the level of self comes praise, which is often used to "comfort and support students." However, just as we saw in teacher stance, praise that is global actually backfires and can lead to negative effects on achievement. As Hattie concludes, "Leave praise out of the feedback about learning" (2012b, 121).

Along with the different levels of feedback, Hattie contends that the most effective feedback narrows the gap between where students are and where they need to be by answering these three questions:

1. Where am I going?
2. How am I going there?
3. And where to next?

As Alisa confers, she zeroes in on those questions, guiding students along their learning journey.

Gradual Release of Responsibility

Vygotsky's research guides our understanding of what it takes to ensure all students have access to challenging curriculum: gradual release of responsibility. Gradual release of responsibility helps teachers figure out how to organize their instruction so that all students will move further along the zone of proximal development to the point where they can apply the skills on their own and independently demonstrate the dispositions needed for challenging work.

In gradual release of responsibility, the responsibility for taking control of the learning is carefully and strategically turned over to the students. Early in the learning as well as throughout the learning process as needed, the lead worker in the classroom is the teacher who assumes the responsibility for showing students how to think through a process or a task. Often done as a think-aloud, the teacher metaphorically opens up her head so the students can listen in on her thinking.

After the modeling, the teacher checks to see if the group understands and determines how much more support they need before they assume more of the role of intellectual worker. Often using the strategies for "total participation" (Himmele and Himmele 2011), teachers check on the understanding of the group. For instance, after modeling how to write a lead to an essay, one teacher we know paired students up to practice. On their portable whiteboards, they wrote a lead to a practice essay and held it up for others to see. Once certain the majority of the class understood, she released more of the responsibility to groups while she moved through the class, conferring with groups.

Frey, Fisher, and Everlove (2009) write extensively about gradual release of responsibility. They argue that the collaborative work, often overlooked, is vital: "Productive group work is an essential stepping stone to learning and mastery" (14). Once again we see the clout of collaboration. As students grow their skills and their confidence to do challenging work, they need to bounce ideas off their peers, muck around together on difficult tasks, hear new perspectives, and collaborate on joint work. This collaboration is necessary for them to eventually be able to work productively independently.

Teachers who understand gradual release of responsibility have a way to think about how to guide those students who need additional support before they're expected to work independently. For students new to English, for instance, the teacher may need to model in more detail the language students need. For students with special learning needs, a teacher may need them to work longer with "more knowledgeable" others before releasing them to work on their own.

Alisa explains how she used gradual release of responsibility for a group of low-performing readers. "I knew that I wanted the same goals for them as I wanted for my other classes, but I knew that I had to slow down to model more and provide more collaborative practice before they could engage in the kind of discourse that would move them. While in my class of higher-performing readers, they might be ready to work independently by mid-September, I knew that I was looking at October for this class. But they'll get there. That's what counts."

Gradual release of responsibility sounds as though it's linear and often is described almost like a formula: I do, we do, you do. However, the model is fluid, all depending on what the students need at that moment. Martha Tudor, a science teacher in Kentucky, had been working with students on using their data to form conclusions. She had modeled, had watched them, and had them work collaboratively. However, when conferring with one student, she noticed his confusion. Quickly, she moved back into the teacher-modeling stage of gradual release: "If it were me, I'd be looking at specific elements of lava. I capture evidence by writing notes on one side. What else might you do?" With this little bit of prompting, he was able to move forward with his thinking.

Alisa, like Martha, sees gradual release of responsibility as fluid even as she plans her learning targets throughout the year. For instance, at the end of each quarter, Alisa decides which learning targets were barely met and which ones students need to dig into once again. Part of this decision is based on checking in with students. She poses questions such as: Which ones are still tricky? When did you feel confident and when did you struggle? In addition to increasing student buy in, she invites students to identify personal learning targets that they will continue working on during a new unit. To do this, she has to push them to track themselves where they are in the moment. Self-reflection is major part of the student's responsibility.

Along with identifying the learning targets the whole class is working on, her responsibility is to create a system for tracking their growth and for reinforcing her commitment to "failure is not an option" (Blankstein 2004).

Strategy 9: Build Autonomy Through Choice

Compliant and shy, Allye did her work, didn't make waves, and almost never talked. Allye was one of those students who seem to fade into the woodwork, a silent teenager who would be easy to overlook. But Kathy Cocetti and Steve Lash knew that her silence had the potential of restricting her growth as a learner and limiting her access to the challenging literature they were reading. Her silence also prevented the class, including Steve and Kathy, from listening to and learning from her insights. They wanted to hear her wrestle with the ideas in the texts they were reading and spar with the authors. Coteachers of Multicultural Literature/World Regional Geography, Kathy and Steve designed the course around student discourse. Discussion, both small group and large group, was a way for students to construct and share knowledge as well as a way for the teachers to assess the understanding of their students.

Every teacher has an Allye in class, and every teacher wrestles with how to bring her voice into the classroom. Sometimes teachers keep calling on the quiet students hoping they will get involved while other teachers ignore those silent ones pleased that they aren't causing trouble and knowing that they can direct their attention to the more vocal students. However, Kathy and Steve were determined to not ignore her but to bring her directly into the learning, making sure that she could access the content under study.

The class was studying the novel *To Live* (2003) by Yu Hua (translated by Michael Berry). For their final assessment, Steve and Kathy could have given students a test and efficiently assessed their understanding. However, they weren't convinced that the test could provide the best avenue for students to demonstrate their understanding. Familiar with multiple intelligences, they decided that Howard Gardner's (2006) ideas might guide them as they designed an assessment that would draw Allye and others into the learning. After giving students a multiple intelligences inventory, they interviewed each student about ways that they might demonstrate their understanding of the novel. When they met with Allye, she talked about her interest in photography and horses. Both Steve and Kathy hoped this approach would capture Allye's imagination and open the doors to hearing her voice.

On the day of the presentations, Allye moved slowly but confidently to her collaborative team where the presentation would take place. She listened to her classmates without saying a word; this did not surprise anyone. Patiently she waited. When it was her turn, she pulled ten photos out of her portfolio. The photos included pictures of her friends enacting critical scenes from the book. The quality of the work immediately caught her classmates' attention, and they leaned forward to get a closer look. Allye went through the photos one by one explaining her connections to the novel. She spoke clearly and confidently in a voice that was new to her peers.

One of Allye's pictures was a pile of horse manure. *To Live* begins with the tale of the dad climbing a pile of manure and, for Allye, this became the metaphor for the entire book. Here's what she wrote:

> "My dad was old and his shit was getting older with him; it was harder and harder to force out" (*To Live*, 9). This quote is not only humorous—referring literally, but metaphorically to what Fugui's father carries around with him. While

I would hope that the literal portion of this excerpt is quite obvious to you . . . metaphorically, Fugui's father really does carry a lot of "shit" with him. He was a gambler, a womanizer, and overall not a very good person, losing a good portion of his family and wealth. And as he gets older, those actions will always stay with him, and there is little he can do to rid himself of it. This can relate to the world we live in today, without our own homes even. If you have done wrong, or misjudged a situation causing a less than desired outcome for yourself or others, other people are going to see that misfortune or wrongdoing every time they come into contact with you.

After Steve heard her presentation, he reflected, "What teacher would have ever steered a kid in this direction? This is the power of choice. Allye was allowed to interpret the meaning of the book in the way she saw it."

Her teammates did not know what to focus on: her confident display of the artistic photos or her insightful interpretation of the novel. Nine weeks into the semester, Allye was heard. "For the first time Allye was comfortable speaking in a small group about something she had learned. The students were amazed and chose her project to be presented to the whole class. Allye displayed her work with pride and confidence. Up to this time, I was not aware of what Allye could bring to the table."

Kathy added, "So here's this person who doesn't speak readily in class, but she could communicate through the visuals she created. She could talk about them; this gave her a chance to really have a voice in the class." Even though it was uncomfortable for Allye to speak up in class, through choice she had a way to access the learning and demonstrate her understandings.

Choice as a Means to Access Challenging Content

All about inspiring passion, not killing it, Kathy Cocetti believes in offering choice whenever possible. What inspired her? She remembers her first time enjoying school. Every Friday Mrs. Greenley would visit her third-grade class to teach reading. "Remember SRA, the Scholastic Reading Achievement program? We had big laminated SRA panels to assess our reading skills and if we got to the colors that were magenta, purple, and blue, you were a good reader. I was always stuck in the yellow and poop-green colors because I wasn't a very good reader." Mrs. Greenley didn't care about labels; she cared about all students accessing literacy.

"Mrs. Greenley had a felt board set up in the classroom and while she read a story to us, she would add characters to the felt board and pick students to take a character or a prop from the story up to the board. I remember thinking 'that's a different way to read.' As a visual learner I could see the story in a different way and understand what was happening." Mrs. Greenley laid the foundation for Kathy. Ever since her exposure to a teacher who knew how to use choice for students to "get it," Kathy has committed thirty years of teaching to using choice as a vehicle to develop student understanding.

"Mrs. Greenley taught me that teaching can be different. It's so important to offer choices to kids; they learn in different ways. You have to value their voice. To me, the most important thing I teach is the importance of having a voice, an actual voice in how I learn. If the kids have a choice, they're going to feel power and they're going to do a better job than if you just prescribe to them."

Kathy puts into practice many of the ideas in *Drive* (Pink 2009). Pink argues that autonomy plays a critical role in motivation. Anyone who works with teens, be it a parent, a teacher, a neighbor, or an employer, knows how important autonomy is for teens, who tend to resist rules, regulations, and mandates. As they transition into adulthood, adolescents insist on—no, demand!—having a say in the events that affect them. Providing choice, even if it's limited choice, is one way teachers can support this need for autonomy and is a powerful way to provide multiple paths of entry into difficult intellectual tasks (Schunk, Pintrich, and Meese 2008). As Kathy said, when students have voice in educational decisions, they are likely to select those routes where they feel confident of success. Interesting that this confidence, this sense of efficacy, actually results in students' exerting more effort and leads to a stronger performance than if they weren't able to have choice:

> According to a cluster of recent behavioral science studies, autonomous motivation promotes greater conceptual understanding, better grades, enhanced persistence at school and in sporting activities, higher productivity, less burnout, and greater levels of psychological well-being. (Pink 2009, 90–91)

And keep in mind what we learn from Carol Dweck. A growth mindset is based on effort. If choice leads to more effort, that one little move on a teacher's part can make a tremendous difference (Dweck 2007).

Think about Allye for a minute. She was a skilled photographer and a lover of horses, and by building from that strength, she was able to demonstrate a sophisticated understanding of the class novel. The time she put into her project far exceeded the time that she would have put into studying for a test or completing a different kind of project that was mandated by the teachers. Her ability to access the content and demonstrate her understanding was dramatically heightened because of choice—and think how much more interesting it is for teachers to grade a variety of work!

A Final Thought

These three strategies—of community, checking in, and choice—provide the foundation for students to access challenging work. John Hattie (2012a) captures the importance of all three of these strategies:

> Feedback thrives in conditions of error or not knowing—not in environments where we already know and understand. Thus teachers need to welcome error and misunderstanding in their classrooms. This attitude, of course, invokes trust. Students learn most easily in an environment in which they can get and use feedback about what they don't know without fearing negative reactions from their peers or their teacher. (23)

If teachers create the kind of classroom community filled with the ethos of caring, they are not mucking around in "touchy feely" stuff that has nothing to do with learning; rather, they're ensuring that students can take those risks that lead to growth. When students go astray in their learning or haven't yet found the path they need to take, feedback matters. And when they know the destination and recognize their strengths and next steps, they are beginning a journey to access difficult, challenging, and important work—work that has the power to transform them and, maybe, even transform their community.

Reflection

LEARNING FROM THE STUDENTS

Consider interviewing two students, one who was successful on a recent assignment and one who was not successful. In the interview, approach the students from a learner's perspective and not from that of an evaluator. In other words, your goal is to understand the students' perspectives about what worked and what the stumbling blocks were. Be sure to ask them about the zones of comfort, risk, and danger to see which zone they were working in throughout the unit.

BLOGGING ABOUT YOUR EXPERIENCES

A professional blog provides teachers a venue for reflecting on their teaching and on their lives as learners. Consider blogging about a critical incident similar to the one that Stevi wrote about at the start of this chapter. Keep in mind that a critical incident is some moment in time the provoked a new insight.

Below are other ideas for the blog:

- When did you learn something that was highly challenging? What did your teacher do or what did you as a learner do that resulted in success?
- When did you NOT learn something that was highly challenging? What could the teacher have done to support you? What could you have done as a learner?
- How do you provide access to difficult learning in your instruction? What else could you do?
- What does gradual release of responsibility look like in your classroom? When did you release students too early or when did you not release them soon enough? What can you learn from those experiences?
- When have you experienced "productive failure"? What conditions were in place for you to grow from that experience? What are the implications for your teaching?

REFLECTING ON YOUR CURRENT PRACTICES

- As you confer with students, record your conversations. Pay close attention to the kind of feedback you offer. How does the feedback close the gap between where they are at that moment in time and where they need to be at the end of the unit? Did you tend to praise effort or was the praise more general?
- Listen for and name the ways that you demonstrate the "power of yet."
- Look at a unit that you've recently taught and note the opportunities you had to check in with students about their learning. Were there opportunities you missed?

EXAMINING AN UPCOMING UNIT

Give yourself some time to refine plans for an upcoming unit. Look at what you have planned and then reflect on the following questions:

- What is nonnegotiable in this unit? For instance, is the unit's major learning goal one of those nonnegotiables? (We would hope that the answer is yes.)
- What is negotiable?
- How can you weave choice into the learning progression? Are there opportunities for students to determine how they might meet a daily learning target? Is there room for choice in reading selections, with selections that are all appropriate to the daily goal?
- How will you know how close students are to meeting the unit's overall goal(s)? When will you provide feedback along the way?

> Failure to prepare is preparing to fail.
>
> —**John Wooden**

CHAPTER 6

Student Access Daily

Teachers in the Spotlight

 Kathy Sampson is a middle school math teacher in Fort Collins, Colorado.

 Lesli Cochran is a middle school humanities teacher whose classroom we've lingered in.

 Alisa Wills-Keely is a high school English teacher whose instructional practices live and breathe "the just-right challenge."

 Ryan Martine is a math coach at the middle school where Kathy Sampson teaches.

As a young aspiring coach, John had the good luck to meet John Wooden, coach of the UCLA men's basketball team that won seven national titles in a row. Curious about the coach's great success, John asked, "How often do you scrimmage during the week before the game?"

Coach Wooden shook his head. "Never." He told John that he needed practice time to work on the small details each player needed: the centers needed work on their big man moves, the forwards on their shot choices, and the guards on reading the defense. (Yes, John Wooden was a teacher.) "When the players were clear about their roles and had the skills, then I knew we were ready for the game."

Wooden's wisdom applies not only to preparing players for basketball games but for preparing all learners to do challenging work. We don't prepare by having them scrimmage but by working on skills needed to succeed at challenging work. Then, we put them into the game.

In this chapter we're going to watch teachers from a variety of subjects prepare their students to participate in the tough game of school. We want you to see what access can look like in very different contexts and how those strategies from Chapter 5 provide that necessary foundation regardless of the age of the student or the subject. You'll sit in on a day in a middle school math teacher's class and then step into the classrooms of the teachers we met in the previous chapter. Kathy and Steve take us through a lesson at the start of a unit filled with challenges, and then we'll figure out how they built their classroom community. We'll return to Alisa Wills-Keely and Lesli Cochran's classrooms to see routines that create access. Then we'll end the chapter with a look at a middle school math department that collectively said, "no more" to restricting access.

Regardless of the content, no matter the academic background of students, none of these teachers just plop students into the game and expect them to do well. Instead, they understand Wooden's advice and thoughtfully design the instruction on a daily basis that will nudge students forward, building those skills and dispositions that will provide access to the tough stuff.

Providing Access Through Routines and Rituals

Kathy Sampson is committed to providing students access to difficult math content. "I know they can get it," she says over and over. "It's up to me to show them how and to create those opportunities." Her stance is clear: students can do challenging math if her instruction is on target. A peek into one day in her classroom is all that it takes to show how she has designed her instruction, including her routines and rituals, so that all students over time will be successful mathematicians. You'll notice that Kathy doesn't let one second of instructional time go to waste. Time is precious, a limited and valued commodity. If she is going to make sure that all students have access to difficult math concepts, she needs to diligently use the time so that every minute counts and students build their confidence and their skills.

Kathy's eighth-grade math class is made up of twenty-seven students of all abilities. She has strong, confident students sitting side by side with students who struggle with math. Recognizing the importance of having strong peer models in the classroom, she wanted a diverse classroom. But because of this mixed-ability room, she was clear that her routines and rituals must provide ways for all students to grow, not leaving some to languish by hiding out or others to yawn in boredom. As you watch her classroom, you'll see how the strategies of community, checking in to move forward, and choice uphold her classroom culture. At the same time, you'll see how her stance of believing in all students shapes her actions.

Her class started with a familiar routine: a problem of the day. Even before the class officially started, students were ready to tackle that problem. Like the other teachers we've described, Kathy has made sure that students know the opening routines of class without her reminding them. They know that during the short time they have to work on the warm-up problem, Kathy will pull up a chair next to several of them, checking in on how they're doing. Strategically, she knew who she would meet with during this time: those students who were likely to have a hard time getting started. Careful not to go to the same students in the same order each day, she used student work, exit cards, and her observations from the previous day to determine who to confer with. She checked in with students to move them forward.

For Kathy, the warm-up is the equivalent of dribbling a ball and shooting hoops to get ready for a basketball game. Muscles need to kick in, and minds need to be attuned to the upcoming work. Kathy's warm-up gets her kids ready to do the work of mathematicians and to practice a bit on some of math procedures that are just emerging, procedures that need more play time.

A Community of Learners Built by Discourse

Toward the end of the warm-up, she wandered over to Dustin's desk and asked if he would work on problem one. At the interactive whiteboard, Dustin wrote his solution to the math problem, explaining this thinking as he jotted down the numbers and calculations. When finished, he turned to the class to see several hands up. He called on Mercedes.

"I noticed that you lined up the decimals. That makes it easier for me to do the problem."

He nodded at Jasmine.

"I noticed that you didn't show all your work."

Kathy, standing to the side of the room, urged Jasmine to elaborate. "Could you explain, Jasmine, why that's an important noticing? Remember we want to extend out thinking."

Jasmine said, "If I show all my work, then I can tell if what I did was right."

For a couple of minutes, Dustin called on a few more students, who all named something they noticed that he did. Each of them extended their thinking by explaining the importance of this noticing.

Clear about the importance of discourse, Kathy made sure that her students had ample opportunities to talk about math. The National Research Council's study on student engagement stresses this importance of talk: "Explaining or teaching something to someone else consolidates and deepens the understanding of the subject matter by the person in the teaching role" (2004, 81). At the same time, other students heard the thinking of their peers, which had the potential of demystifying math concepts for those who were still early in their understanding. But talk also serves another important function. It builds a sense of community—a group united by discourse, a social network that linked all the individuals in the class together.

Kathy didn't want just any talk; she wanted her students to talk like mathematicians and in a respectful manner. To ensure that students knew how to engage in such discourse, she taught them routines for math conversations. As a reminder on her wall was a poster with sentence starters:

- I agree with _____ because _____
- I disagree with _____ because _____
- I started my problem by _____, and then I _____
- I have a question: _____
- I noticed that _____
- This is the same as _____ because _____
- This is different from _____ because _____
- I solved the problem differently by _____
- My answer is _____ because _____

It's important to note that this poster was not just decoration. It was used by students and by Kathy. Now and then throughout the class, some students would turn to the poster for a reminder of how to begin a conversation. When Kathy needed to nudge students to extend their thinking, she casually pointed in the direction of the poster.

Teacher as Model

Transitioning from the warm-up to the new learning of the day, Kathy explained, "Let me tell you about the kind of problems that we're going to be working with today. You'll see from the learning targets that our focus is on uniform motion and multiple representations of problems. Watch me while I think through this problem."

Thinking aloud is a common practice in her classroom. As we saw in Chapter 2 when Emily showed her science students her thinking, a think-aloud is a way for a teacher to open up her head and let students eavesdrop on her thinking. Students have the chance to watch an expert wrestle with challenges, noting how sometimes thinking takes a circuitous route while the teacher models the struggles and the success.

In Kathy's think-aloud, she wanted to show her students her thinking routines when she encountered a word problem: "As a mathematician, the first thing I do is read. I want to pull out the things that are important." She read the problem to them, occasionally pausing to show her thinking. "Right now I'm sharing my thinking with you. I go straight to the 'find' part of the problem because that will let me know the variables that I'm searching for." After reading a bit further, she paused again. "Now I know that I have to find the rates, so I'm going to underline this. I'm thinking about a ratio and know that I have to figure that ratio out."

She stopped thinking aloud and turned to the class, "This is as far as I'm going to go. You'll have a similar problem. Remember our learning target says to go after multiple representations, so your task—and your challenge—is to find different ways to represent the problem. Right now I want you to talk to your group. Read the problem and find the variables you need to pay attention to. Then brainstorm the multiple ways that you might represent the problem. Remember, one way won't cut it. Find others."

This task mirrored the findings of the National Research Council's study of engagement. Math students in classes where the engagement was high often were given regularly "open ended problems that had multiple solutions or strategies" (2004, 82). Even though Kathy suspected that students might represent the problem in several predictable ways—multiple-step equation, a rate table, guess and check, a graph, a ratio—she was curious to see if new possibilities would emerge and knew that choice would push their thinking.

Along with offering students a substantial task, Kathy wanted to make sure that students collaborated, another means for providing access to challenging content (National Research Council 2004). Frequently, she changed the membership of the groups in order to ensure that students knew each other well and, therefore, to strengthen their classroom community. She made certain that those students who struggled in math worked side by side with more skilled students. To make sure the mixed-ability grouping worked for all, she taught students how to collaborate, stressing the importance of turn taking and checking in regularly with each other. She knew that if she didn't show them the social skills for effective collaboration, it was unlikely that the groups would make a difference in the learning (Quate and McDermott 2009; Chiu 2008).

Checking in to Move Forward: Conferring

As the students began working on the new set of problems in their groups, Kathy moved from group to group. At the start of the class, she conferred with individuals, but now she conferred with groups, stressing the importance of all of them contributing to the learning of each other. Her questions followed a predictable pattern beginning with "How are we doing?" As she listened to the group talk, she probed their thinking:

- "Can you tell me more?"
- "What other information do you need?"
- "Why do you care?"
- "What difference does it make?"

When the group presented a solution, she would paraphrase: "So you're doing a graph. Tell me more." Often she would check if this was one person talking or the thinking of the group:

- "Do you all agree?"
- "Who has another way of doing this?"

Kathy's stance for conferring was not to monitor their behavior or their cooperation. Instead, she saw herself as the coach, the person who would nudge them to think further and the person to ensure that the collaborative work of the group was leading to each person in the group getting smarter about math. She urged them to think from a variety of perspectives and use the language of math. She also put into practice Hattie's three questions (2012b) for powerful feedback that we discussed in Chapter 5: Where am I going, how am I going there, and where to next?

In one group, she noted that two of the students were on the right track, but the third one wasn't. On top of that, all three were working independently. When she conferred with them, she checked on their understanding of the task and on the ways that they chose to represent the information. But because she knew that they were not effectively working as a group, she prompted them to work with each other and stay with a problem until all three of them were confident about their representations. Not long after she left them, the dynamics of the group shifted. One student leaned across the table and showed the struggling student how to do the task. The third student looked over both tablemates' calculations to see if they were in synch. This was a striking example of the strategy of checking in to move forward in their learning!

While conferring, she noted where groups as well as the class as a whole needed more guidance. Every now and then, she would catch the attention of the class to quickly comment: "If you find the answer, great. Find another way to represent it. Look at that learning target and remember that it's multiple representation that I'm looking for." And then she quickly released them back to their work.

As Kathy rotated around the room, she looked for students whose thinking seemed particularly strong. She invited them to share their thinking with the rest of the class. Through this invitation, she gave students plenty of time to get ready for their explanation. They were able to rehearse what they would say and double-check that their content was right. This invitation wasn't just for those students who were academically strong but for all ranges of ability and skill levels. This was just one more routine that built access through classroom community.

Over and over the impact of a strong classroom community could be seen in Kathy's room. Students were encouraged to take risks and to try something new. When students presented problems with errors or misconceptions, she congratulated them on their thinking and efforts and used the occasion as a way to talk through their misunderstandings. Near the end of class, Jasmine went to the whiteboard and drew a graph as one way to represent the data. Instead of labeling the horizontal axis x, she mislabeled it as y. As she worked at the interactive whiteboard, Kathy urged her to explain her procedures. Kathy gently probed her about her thinking about labeling the two axes and encouraged the rest of the class to think along with Jasmine about how to make those decisions. Stressing the importance of not knowing for sure, they talked and talked, eventually clarifying the concept. Once again, these routines in her classroom reflect the findings of the National Research Council: "Opportunities to talk about mathematical problems with others appears to benefit students only when the teacher skillfully focuses the discourse squarely on mathematics, establishing norms that uncertainty is good and is a prerequisite for complex reasoning" (2004, 83).

Risk taking was honored, and mistakes were celebrated as ways to grow smarter in Kathy's room.

Access Through Choice and Community

Like Kathy Sampson, Steve Lash and Kathy Cocetti (the co-teachers from Chapter 5) have strong routines and rituals in place that ensure their sophomores can access challenging content. Kathy and Steve live the first two strategies of access through the caring classroom community of learners and checking in with their students to move them forward. However, their strategy of choice is where these two teachers shine the brightest. Clearly, they understood the strategy of building autonomy through choice. A look at how they co-taught Shakespeare's *Othello* shows the power of those routines and rituals. The play wasn't one either teacher would have selected, but one they had to teach because of a departmental decision. They knew that this play was going to be quite daunting for their students. Kathy explained, "Right from the beginning we knew we were going to have to include choice to get the kids hooked into this play." If they didn't figure out a hook, they would have a long month ahead of them.

Ways to Add Choice

Like Lesli Cochran's decision in teaching a Shakespearean play (see Chapter 5), their first task was to determine what that hook would be. To do that, they had to figure out what would stump students right from the start. They realized that if students couldn't make sense of the language and struggled with the pronunciation of some of the words, they'd never be able to interpret the play. As they brainstormed the many difficulties and possible entry points, Steve hit on the solution: *Seinfeld*. "Remember that episode where the characters played with different pronunciations of the line, 'These pretzels are making me thirsty'? That's what we'll have them do."

Moving the students into heterogeneous groups of three, they gave the students the task. Out of twenty dialogues in act 1, the groups had to select one to perform and then explain the significance of the scene it was in. But the kicker was that they had to interpret the lines three different ways, and the class would vote on the best of the three.

The energy in the room was high as students rose to the challenge.

"So, what do you think that word means?"

"Let's look it up."

"What else must be going on in act 1 if he is saying this line?"

"You keep working on the line, and I'll read what was happening before he said it."

One Thursday afternoon John dropped by their class as they were arguing about a scene in *Othello*. About fifty students in this team-taught class were in the room. Often Steve and Kathy merged the two classes together so the numbers were high, but despite the large number of students, all were engaged. Even though the students had never met John before, he was welcomed into the conversation as if he had been an old friend. You see, when the caring classroom is established and the students are accustomed to collaborating with each other, another learner added to the group is, well, simply another opportunity to learn.

Ways to Add Choice

At the close of the lesson, and with no coaching or review of his project, John asked Kathy's students the value of choice in the classroom.

June, one of Kathy's students who needed a little push now and then, described the difference choice made in her learning. "As a not-so-motivated student, when Ms. Cocetti gives us the option to choose how we learn, not only is it just a nice change of pace from the regular multiple-choice test but it makes me feel more responsible and in control of my education."

Another student explained the many ways they had been offered choice so far in the year. "You should have seen the crepe paper stained-glass window one group made to show how they interpreted a scene from a book we read. And after Ms. Cocetti told us about some sidewalk-chalk images she saw in Italy, another student picked up on her idea and that's how she showed us her understanding. Some other students wrote poems and songs. It was cool to watch the presentations." When pushed to explain the purpose of each of these activities, the student was able to name the specific learning target: to connect a scene to the larger theme of the book, to interpret a character's actions, to analyze an author's choice of words and how that choice supports the overall meaning of the text. Each of these learning targets were directly connected to the Common Core State Standards.

A student sitting near John added, "Limiting choice is like limiting the potential of the student. The more choice the student is offered, the greater their possibilities of succeeding. But it's important for us to also know the purpose of our work. Otherwise, it can feel like busywork."

Steve explained how they planned for choice. "This was the best thing we did in our planning stages. We really took on how we were going to assess students throughout the unit and figured out what we wanted them to do at the very end. After we figured out the standards our unit addresses, we looked at each other and said, 'OK, how will we do these things, but in a cool way?' Many of their choices reflected the strategy of authenticity so it was work that could be found in the world outside of school, work similar to what an artist, a musician, a reader, or a writer might actually engage in." Steve continued, "We were not going to do paper-and-pencil tests to demonstrate knowledge at the end of every unit. Talk about a great way to kill anyone's passion for literacy!"

What was not negotiable was the learning target; what was negotiable was how students reached the target and demonstrated mastery (Quate and McDermott 2009). All those daily choices over time resulted in high engagement:

- When possible, students had a choice of text. For instance on some days, students might read a poem, a story, or a short essay about the theme under study.
- During work time, students often had the choice of working independently or with a partner.
- When students annotated text, they determined what was important to think about and why.
- When students moved into groups, they often decided which text or which quote they would bring to the group discussion.
- When there were several essential questions, students determined which ones they would explore.
- When the learning target was open enough for students to determine how they would demonstrate their understanding, they would decide if they would represent mastery through a creative presentation or through a more traditional route.

Choice was rampant in their classroom but always purposeful and directly connected to an academic goal.

The Clout of Community

Why were students so eager to engage in this challenge? Kathy and Steve had carefully nurtured a caring classroom community throughout the year. They made sure that students knew the first and last names of their classmates, and as they collaborated on projects, they established norms for group work. Regularly they made positive phone calls home to let parents know the hard work their students were doing (Quate and

McDermott 2009). The community of the classroom was strong and provided the clout needed for students to take risks and grow.

Checking in to Move Forward: Feedback

Kathy and Steve take assessment seriously. They know the power of assessment that is done well. Applying the research of Black et al. (2003), they not only clarify the criteria for assessing student learning but also bring students into the assessment process. Students co-create rubrics and regularly self-assess, figuring out where they are, where they're going, and what to do next to get closer to the goal.

Feedback trumps grading in terms of growing learners (Black et al. 2003). Already in the first nine weeks of the year, Steve and Kathy had offered a plethora of feedback about student writing, reading, and classroom understanding. They filled student papers with comments that provided feedback, but it is worth noting that their comments were on drafts, so students still had time to incorporate the feedback. Because these teachers know that comments on graded papers are often ignored—except, perhaps, by motivated, academically secure students—they shared personal stories in them and prompted students to think about how others might react to the issues. They nudged students forward by showing them how to close the gap between where their writing was at that moment and where it could be in the near future.

Access Through Scaffolding

As we've seen, Lesli Cochran has powerful routines and rituals that not only reveal her stance (see Chapters 1 and 2) but also provide students access to challenging content. One of her routines is showing her students how to think while reading and writing. She regularly checked in with them to assess where they were in their understanding. Based on those check-ins, she figured out the scaffolding that would best support their learning. Scaffolding is the perfect metaphor for what she does. In the process of building her students' understanding, Lesli constructed a temporary support, intended to be removed, just like the scaffolding that surrounds a building under construction

It was not only the routines and rituals but also the scaffolding that led to success in all Lesli's classes. Most of her students not only had strong grades but also had some of the school's highest scores on the state's assessment. Nevertheless, for many, it was the first time in middle school that they were convinced they could access difficult intellectual content. Lesli was certain that her routine of focusing on both content and process made the difference: "I can't tell them to just read and make inferences about the text. I have to show them how to infer, how to think, and then I have to make sure they have plenty of practice in doing that kind of thinking."

Often at the start of the year her students viewed reading as a passive activity and crossed their fingers that what they read would stick, like Velcro. When they struggled with making meaning of text, they believed it was simply that they were not as smart as the girl in the other row who seemed to just plain get it. To combat the view of reading as passive, Lesli structured her minilessons around the thinking strategies of proficient readers (Tovani 2000, 2004). To demystify the reading/thinking process, she named those cognitive strategies, modeled them, and supported students as they practiced them. Typically she would spend a couple of weeks building students' background knowledge about the strategies; however, the group of students we described in Chapter 1 needed more support. "As I was conferring, too many of these guys just sat there when they were stuck in their reading, or they faked it. Even after a couple weeks of work with them, they were relying too much on me to figure out the meaning of the book."

Lesli worried that the labels these students carried with them into the classroom led to their lack of efficacy. Convinced of their fixed ability, they had little hope that their efforts would pay off, so being passive or a class goof-off reaped more rewards than exerting the effort to succeed academically. Lesli's description of her students mirrored Dweck's research: students who believe ability trumps effort rely heavily on the teacher. Lacking in confidence and skills, they are easily stumped and retreat quickly, waving the white flag for help. Lesli was determined to shift that mindset and build a sense of competency, but that required scaffolding, more than what she often needed to provide for students.

Effective scaffolding follows the Goldilocks principle: not too much, not too little, but just the right amount. Clearly, if she offered too much support, she would reinforce students' perceptions of themselves as lacking intellectual gusto, but if she didn't offer enough support, students would flounder. It had to be just right—and just right for the individuals in her classroom, not some idealized version. Figure 6.1 shows examples of effective scaffolds.

Figure 6.1: Examples of Scaffolds

- Anchor Charts
- Chunking a complex task or a complex text into manageable parts
- Flip Books
- Graphic Organizers
- Magic Cards of Fate
- Sentence Starters
- Think-Alouds
- Verbal Cues
- Word Walls

Figure 6.2: Lesli's Flip Book

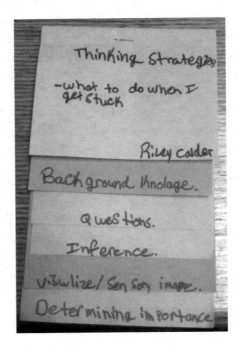

Because of the support this group of kids needed, Lesli designed a flip book that listed each of the thinking strategies.

She explained, "Whenever they got stuck, they had to go to the first page and do what it said: activate background knowledge. And if that didn't help them get unstuck, their task was to flip to the second page and ask questions. I needed them to be more independent than what they were. So when I conferred I used the flip book until I saw that they were doing that kind of thinking on their own."

The flip books were a regular part of the classroom for the first quarter of the year. By the second quarter, students no longer needed them, and gradually the flip books disappeared from view. Like any good scaffolding, when the job was done, the scaffolding disappeared.

Scaffolding Through Invitational Minilessons

Alisa Wills-Keely realized that there were times when some students simply didn't meet the learning target and needed more support. A few years ago, she hit on the idea of the invitational minilesson designed for a particular group of students, not the entire class.

Figure 6.3: Magic Cards of Fate

Gerardo Munoz, a teacher in the Denver Center of International Studies, scaffolds discourse through the "magic cards of fate." At the beginning of the school year, he has students write their names on cards. He keeps those cards on his desk, and when students are about to engage in a whole class discussion, he pulls out the "magic cards of fate."

Those whose names are on the cards are responsible for answering the questions. Sometimes he'll place the names he pulled at the bottom of the cards while other times he places the names back in the stack and then shuffles them, making sure that no one can escape the randomness of being called on.

At the start of class, she would announce the topic of the invitational minilesson, invited all interested students to join her, then issue a personal invitation to the few students most in need of that lesson at that exact moment. Not all invitational mini-lessons were planned, however. Sometimes they were impromptu in order to address an urgent need. During work time, she would catch the students quickly: "Because I've noticed several of you are having problems in this one area, I'm going to do an invitational minilesson on this topic in about five minutes. If you're busy and in flow, keep working. The rest of you can join me in the back corner of the room. Be sure to bring your notebooks."

Alisa is convinced that the invitational minilessons, both the ones planned based on the previous day's work and those that are more spontaneous, have met the goal of ensuring that all students with the appropriate amount of support could meet her challenging goals.

Within a School: Flexible Grouping

Throughout this chapter, we've looked at individual teachers' routines and rituals that enable students to gain access to knowledge that at one time might have been out of their reach. Some schools have also thought about systems beyond the classroom that either prevent or lead to student access. One such school is Preston Middle School in Fort Collins, Colorado. For the last several years, Preston's math department has implemented a system that provides all students more time and more opportunities to become skillful, confident mathematicians.

Preston Middle School sits at the edge of Fort Collins. The school is remarkably different from the schools where Negar, Emily, Jennifer, and Lesli teach. Unlike their schools, Preston's students come from a middle-class setting, and the school's performance on the state assessment has been solidly strong. Despite those results, there is an attitude that resounds through the school: we can and we will do better.

Addressing the Barriers

Ryan Martine, Preston's math coach, was passionate about studying the data from the school's formal assessments. On a quick read, it appeared that in math students were doing well. But as he began digging more deeply into the data, he noted a clear achievement gap. Students in the advanced math classes did impressively well, outscoring those students in regular or low math classes. As he pondered the implications of the gap, he wondered if the system of tracking was the culprit.

Under his leadership, the department studied the research on tracking. They saw that students in high tracks were expected to think critically, solve problems, and engage in rich conversations. In contrast, students in the lower track tended to work independently with little collaboration or discourse. In addition, in the lower-tracked classes students did not see someone their age working through tough problems or persevering through challenging work, so they had no positive role models. Much of their work involved worksheets that "skilled and drilled" them on lower-level skills (Martino 2012). The Preston teachers wanted more for their students. With the blessing of their principal, they decided to develop a new system where all students would take higher-level math classes, including Algebra 1. The eighth-grade team opted to keep one higher-level math class for those students who had successfully completed Algebra 1.

And so they changed the system and detracked most of their math classes, moving all students into high levels of math. The math teachers carefully studied student performance. As they predicted, some students were more confident and skilled as mathematicians while others struggled. They saw three groups emerge: those flying high with upper-level math who needed more challenge, those right on track, and those in need of more support. They had removed one barrier to access for challenging math, but new challenges presented obstacles to face, problems to solve, new systems to develop. They knew they had to figure this out since they were not willing to go back to the days of tracking.

In their research, they encountered the research of Diane Heacox (2009) and Carol Ann Tomlinson (2004), two leading advocates of differentiation. Tomlinson reminded them of an important learning point: "We fail students when we assume that they learn in the same way and in accordance with a singular time table" (521). As they studied her research, they saw they had two choices: differentiation within the classroom and differentiation between classrooms. Both options were viable. Within the classroom, teachers committed to differentiation, and as a department they wanted to figure out how to differentiate between classrooms, knowing that to do so they had to coordinate their plans and their learning targets if this was going to work. For additional support, Ryan dedicated time to work with each of the grade-level teams.

Like Alisa, they defined differentiation as providing multiple ways for students to meet common and specific learning targets. So in grade teams, the teachers planned the week's learning targets and designed the assessments. Coordinating with Ryan's schedule, each grade selected a different day to differentiate, called a flexible grouping day. Prior to the flexible grouping day, the teachers taught their lessons, working with small groups and coaching individuals. On their predetermined day, they administered another assessment. Based on that data, they determined how students would be grouped the following day: enrichment or extension, on target, or support.

When students walked into their regular math classes on their day for flexible grouping, they learned what room they would move to, and for that class period, students received the instruction needed to move them toward (or beyond) their learning targets. Since each block was eighty minutes long, they had at least sixty minutes of learning, even with the time needed to move the students into their rooms for the day. Ryan joined one of the groups, usually the one with the students who needed additional support, in the role of co-teacher. When students returned to their regular class, they reflected on the work that they had done, sharing with others what they had learned and what a difference the experience made in their growth as mathematicians.

It wasn't long before students came to rely on and appreciate these days. Sue Martino, a seventh-grade math teacher voted regional math teacher of the year, studied flexible grouping for her master's thesis. In her thesis, Sue argued that by flexibly grouping students among classrooms that the department was systematically able to provide more time and more opportunities for students to become skillful, confident mathematicians. Students noted that math was both challenging and accessible. Because of the support, their confidence that they could succeed grew. In her surveys of students, she noted that many students appreciated that teachers recognized and responded to their different needs. One student in an enrichment class commented, "In the beginning I felt confident because I could make the tables. But then I had a tough time because of the graphing. I was challenged most of the time, but liked the challenge because it wasn't easy." Another student, not as skilled in math, commented about the flexible groups, "We get to go at our pace, so we can learn. We don't get in a group where we don't know anything" (Martino 2012, 17).

And the results? Impressive! After one year of flexible grouping, Preston's math scores zoomed upward. In fact, they had the one of the state's highest "growth" scores on the math state assessment. Students who had been average or below average in the past showed an average of a year and a half's growth (Martino 2012). After the second year, again the data from the assessment showed a marked difference. The growth of all groups—economically disadvantaged, English language learners, students with disabilities—was close to the overall growth. Students were scoring well. But along with the data, the teachers learned from surveys and interviews with the students that their confidence in math had increased as well as their enjoyment.

Same Ol'? Same Ol'?

Some teachers worried that flexible grouping would end up being a disguised version of the "bluebirds and robins" like the old days of tracking with the same students in enrichment week after week and the same students in the extra-help group week after week. What they found calmed those fears: the membership of the flexible groups varied weekly. As Martino noted, "Students do not always need the same level of support or enrichment from week to week" (2012, 4). Students caught on faster to some concepts than to others. Martino looked carefully at how varied the flexible groups actually were. She learned that no student remained in the support group each week and that all students who scored poorly on the state assessment had the chance to work with two different groups. She concluded: "Flexible grouping by readiness and academic performance is not a fixed and permanent arrangement for students." With this changing demographic on a weekly basis, the teachers were able to remove any kind of worry of limiting the opportunities and resources for any group of students.

Sue sums it up: "We are instilling the belief that all students can learn and think at a high level."

Back to Wooden

Each of these teachers and the Preston Middle School math department shared John Wooden's belief in getting students ready for the game. They also reflected on another "Woodenism": Failing to prepare is preparing to fail. In their planning and in the smart ways they built their classroom communities, they provided access to challenging content, opening up doors for all and making sure that no student was shut out of the learning.

Window into Practice: After

As you read the following vignette describing Ms. Johnson a few months after the vignette that opened Part 3, what do you notice? How has she provided access to the challenging work? What made the difference in the students' attitudes toward the class?

Two months after the assessment of the essays, Ms. Johnson's class looked and sounded different. Ahmad was still in the back of the room, but he was with two other students discussing the song he wrote about Okonkwo's trouble. Frank was sharing his ideas from a drawing representing the missionaries in *Things Fall Apart*. Marissa was leading her coaching team's discussion. The class knew that they were working toward the major learning goal of the unit: I can synthesize the big ideas of *Things Fall Apart* in an essay in order to convince the reader that the novel's themes either are or are not relevant to today's life.

Daily their learning targets led them to writing that essay, and daily students had choice in how to demonstrate meeting those learning targets. As usual, Ms. Johnson was checking in with students by asking questions to home in on student interpretations of Okonkwo's plight. "I see what you are saying about the effect of the missionaries, but what do you understand the author to be saying?"

She moved to Ahmad. "Ahmad, what was most confusing about organizing your thoughts for the song? How did our questioning techniques help you make sense of the reading?"

Ms. Johnson interrupted the sharing that was going on in small groups. "I want to hear you using the sentence stems from the board as you ask probing questions about the reading. Those who have not completed last night's reading, go ahead to the 'quiet corner,' catch up, and then rejoin your coaching team."

"OK," Ms. Johnson stopped the conversations. "Now that you had a choice in how you represented the reading, and you collaborated with your coaching teams, I want you to grab a marker, go to the chart paper hanging around the room, and write down possible thesis statements for your essay."

The students were up and moving with multiple ideas for writing.

As the students returned to their seats, Ms. Johnson encouraged them, "Once you have a thesis, just write! Write your ideas; let them flow in your first draft. Use your 'choice' assignments and your coaching team discussions to guide your thinking. You will have multiple opportunities to revise. This is what writers do!"

Ahmad, Frank, and Marissa came to class with rough drafts of their thinking. Ahmad mused, "I learned it's OK to make mistakes as long as I am willing to learn from them and correct them."

Marissa added, "We still do a lot of writing, but I feel I have more control over what and how I write this essay."

Frank concluded, "It's weird. I actually like this class now."

Growing Impatient

Here we are, challenged with meeting the needs of thousands of Justins, Jerardos, Maggies, and Connors. We need to usher these students into the game and make sure they're ready to play. We must embody a teacher stance embedded in a belief that all students are capable of doing the challenging work that they deserve. We can and must create learning environments filled with pressing, transformative, and authentic work. We have to provide access to all learners.

We all know how daunting this call is, but it must be done—now. The big ideas in our book are far from radical; instead, we wanted to show how a few shifts in our teaching can yield tremendous results. Reflecting on our stance, ensuring that we offer work that matters, and being mindful of the ways we can provide access to all students can build the classrooms that our students deserve, classrooms that will grow them as thinkers, as citizens, and as moral human beings.

Unfortunately, we still walk into classrooms and see teachers lecturing while the students sit quietly taking notes—not once in a while, but every day. We hear teachers trying to remember the names of students in the second quarter of the year. We hear teachers saying to students, "No, you cannot revise your work. This is the real world!" We see students stuck in tracked systems, being denied the challenging work they deserve. We see students with special needs still ostracized from the regular classroom. We hear teachers say, "I don't do group work; it's a waste of time and too chaotic." We peek into classrooms where the walls do not reflect students' cultures and interests. We see teachers focusing on students' deficits instead of celebrating their assets. We see students denied choice and voice.

Fortunately we also spend time with teachers in schools and classrooms like yours who are doing this work. We watched Lesli pour her heart and soul into making sure all her students know what good readers do. Yes, even students labeled as struggling and difficult. Lesli believed they could read and provided the conditions for them to do so. We sat with Jennifer and Negar as they took their urban students to the edge of their capacity to do the work of mathematicians and literary scholars. We applauded the efforts of Kathy Sampson, Emily Skrobko, Alisa Wills-Keely, Steve Lash, Kathy Cocetti, Sue Martino, and Ryan Martine as they did everything in their power to make sure their students could access difficult content.

The teachers we write about are real. Their environments are real, and they face the same challenges every teacher in this country faces. They deal with a state legislature that passes laws that are the antithesis of what teachers believe in. In their schools they face scripted, regimented curriculums that emphasize rigor instead of vigor. They face administrations that are stripped of funding and bullied by political parties bereft of critical thinking. And they face the pressure to conform.

What do they do? Lesli, Emily, Kathy, and Alisa follow routines and rituals designed to provide scaffolding for every learner. Negar and Jennifer keep pressing their students to learn, even though their schools are being closed by the state in the name of advancing education. Kathy and Steve work under a curriculum guide designed to standardize content for a diverse student population. Sue and Ryan work to change a tracked system and create a new one where no one is denied access to high-level math.

These teachers will not back down.

Stop for one minute and think about your most recalcitrant or compliant learners. What do you really believe about your students? Do you really believe they are capable of excellence? Of growth? Of being intellectuals? If you believe this, what do your words and actions indicate to these students?

Think about your classroom. Is the work worthy of your students? Is it work that matters? Are your students routinely asked to problem-solve and think critically about important, relevant issues? Do you spend your classroom time ensuring that students are engaged in high-level thinking directly related to their lived experiences?

Are you providing multiple pathways for students to access challenging content? Do your routines and rituals provide opportunities for all students to succeed? Do you teach your students how to collaborate? Are your students an integral part of the assessment process? Do your students have choices in their learning? Do they have a voice?

These are things we can control.

Just like all the teachers in this book, we have students enter our classrooms with a defiant stance of "Here I am, so try and teach me." We know how challenging our job can be. However, these challenges must not prevent us from providing the kind of education filled with opportunities for all students to succeed. Teachers know what needs to be done.

As John Wooden preached to his players, "Do not let what you cannot do interfere with what you can do" (ESPN 2010). The teachers in this book have shown us what can be done.

Teachers, you control how you teach even as the pressures to conform permeate our profession. John's fifth-grade teacher, Sister Martin, taught him a lesson that has stuck. She would look at the thirty-some students in our class and say, "Wrong is wrong if everybody's wrong and right is right if nobody is right."

We cannot keep waiting for someone else to tackle the wrongs in our profession. We need to start doing what is right, and every teacher knows what has to be done. Call it the six Cs, call it best practices, call it whatever you like; all students need to be challenged and supported in a safe environment.

This work needs to be done.

We grow impatient.

And so do our students.

And so do you.

Take some risks.

Students can't wait.

Appendix

Protocols for Student Discussion

Listening to the Author

1. After reading the article, find a quote that sparkles—something that you think is particularly well written, contains a provocative idea, or captures the essence of the article.

2. Read around—each person reads his/her selected quote without making any comment about why it was selected. Read the quote even if someone else has read it before. (It's most interesting to hear quotes repeated.)

3. Just listen to the words of the author as your group reads their quotes. Soak in the ideas.

4. Once everyone has read their quote, discuss the selected quotes. Begin the discussion with this question: What did we hear?

5. Possible follow-up questions:

    a. What was missing? What did we not hear that we might have?

    b. How were our quotes similar? Dissimilar?

    c. What surprised us?

    d. How did the "read around" influence our understanding of the text?

Save the Last Word for Me

1. Write a significant quote from the text on one side of the index card. The quote should resonate with the reader, perhaps stating an idea that the reader agrees with or strongly disagrees with.

2. On the back of the card, explain the significance of the quote.

3. One student at a time reads the quote and points to where in the text this quote can be found. The student does not explain its significance.

4. The rest of the group discusses this quote.

5. The first student reads the back of the card or explains the significance of the quote. In other words, this person gets *the last word*.

6. Move on to the next student until everyone in the group has had a chance to have the last word.

Four As Text Protocol

1. The group reads the text silently, highlighting it and writing notes in the margin or on sticky notes in answer to the following four questions:

    • What *Assumptions* does the author of the text hold?

    • What do you *Agree* with in the text?

- What do you want to *Argue* with in the text?
- What parts of the text do you want to *Aspire* to?

2. In a round, have each student identify one assumption in the text, citing the text (with page numbers, if appropriate) as evidence. After hearing each assumption, the group discusses the assumptions.
3. The group talks about the text in light of each of the remaining As, taking them one at a time—what do people want to argue with, agree with, and aspire to in the text?
4. End the session with an open discussion framed around a question such as: What does this mean for our studies?

Three Levels of Text Protocol

1. Have students sit in a circle and identify a facilitator/timekeeper.
2. If students have not done so ahead of time, have them read the text and identify passages (and a couple of backups) that they feel may have important connections to their current studies (i.e., the unit theme, the author study, the genre study).
3. A round consists of one person using up to three minutes to:
   a. LEVEL 1: Read aloud the passage she/he has selected.
   b. LEVEL 2: Say what she/he thinks about the passage (interpretation, connection to past experiences, etc.).
   c. LEVEL 3: Say what she/he sees as the implications of the passage to what is currently being studied in class. (This level is at the application level of thinking.)
   d. The group responding (for a TOTAL of up to two minutes) to what has been said.
4. Move on to the next person.

Tuning Protocol for Writing Tasks

Roles

1. *Facilitator:* The person who guides the conversation and ensures that the steps are followed exactly as described here; this role should change for each presentation.
2. *Timekeeper:* The person who monitors the time and reminds participants when time is up; this role should rotate.
3. *Writer:* The writer presents her draft for feedback. It's best if she has made copies for everyone.
4. *Responders:* The people who listen carefully to the writer, read her piece carefully, and provide feedback; they need to also consider what lessons they can gain from listening to and discussing the work of others.

Steps

1. The first writer explains what her intention is for the piece, poses a question that she would like the group to help her think about, and then reads her paper aloud to the group. (5 minutes)
2. The responders *ask clarifying questions*. These are factual questions that are intended to help the responders understand the work and the writer's question. (3 minutes)

AT THIS POINT THE WRITER MOVES OUT OF THE GROUP. SHE TAKES NOTES BUT MAY NOT PARTICIPATE IN THE DISCUSSION.

3. The *responders discuss* what they have heard. (8 minutes)
   a. Warm or positive comments: What are the strengths of what they heard and read? Where is the voice particularly strong? What are the lines that resonate with the readers? (Note: these are only sample questions.)
   b. Cool, NOT cruel, comments: What questions are there? What are other possibilities? What do you wonder about in terms of their work? Where does the work not quite hold together? What are other options for the writer?

   In this discussion, it's important to attend to the question the writer posed. Also it's wise to apply the focus lessons to this writing.

4. The writer returns to the group and *talks about what she learned from the feedback*. This is a time to explore interesting ideas that came out of this experience. (4 minutes)
5. Continue this process with the next writer.

Ways to Learn About Students and Their Cultures

Cultural Maps

Rationale

- Cultural maps offer an explanation of culture encompassing a broad spectrum definition.
- Cultural maps allow students to brainstorm a list of important cultural traits, events, places, clothing, music, and people who are important in their lives.
- Cultural maps provide a way for teachers to understand the cultures of their students.

Steps in Creating a Cultural Map

1. Create your own cultural map to use as an exemplar.
2. Have students brainstorm important cultural traits, events, places, clothing, music, and people.

3. Encourage students to organize their thoughts into a theme.
4. Give them paper, markers, and time to create.
5. Provide a checklist or rubric to guide students in their creation.
6. Get out of the way.
7. Display their work in the classroom.
8. Conduct a discussion about the results.
9. Have the students generate answers to this question: Based on this information, what should I incorporate into my units, lessons?

Personal Philosophy Statements and Goal Statements

In order to discover the best educational environment for your students, you need to continue learning about their needs throughout the school year. Think about having your students write personal philosophy statements to find out what they believe about life, learning, and their future. Let them play with this process and revisit and revise their thinking as the school year progresses.

Simultaneously, allow your students to write goal statements for the short and long term. Adjust your instruction based on your knowledge of student needs.

Ideas for Collaboration

Coaching Partners

Assign each student a coaching partner. Several times during the class period have the coaching partners meet to summarize the lesson and to quiz each other on the content. The goal of the coaching partner is to ensure their buddy learns the content.

Pair/Share with Accountability

Before you begin, write each student's name on a three-by-five-inch card.

- In pairs, have students answer questions or solve a problem. Do not give them too much time to do this.
- Shuffle the cards and draw a student's name. This is the person who answers the question or states the solution.
- Return the card to the deck, and shuffle again. (It's important to put the card back because it's the randomness of the card selection that counts. Students need to feel like their name could be called at any time and that there is no such thing as getting off the hook.)

Triads

When the goal is for students to think at high levels, triads may provide access to the learning. Ask the students to form groups of three. Once students are in triads, pose a challenging question. Set the timer to two minutes. When the buzzer goes off, have students form a new group of three, but they cannot meet with anyone from their previous group. Pose a new challenging question and set the timer. This continues for one more rotation. Have students return to their seats and randomly call on students to respond to any of the questions.

Inner Outer Circle

Remind the class about the skills of being a good listener: appropriate body language, eye contact, not speaking until the speaker has finished, the role of clarifying questions.

Number off by twos. The "ones" form a circle standing shoulder to shoulder facing outward. The "twos" find a partner from the "ones" and face them. You now have two concentric circles.

Designate one of the circles as the listeners and one of the circles as the speakers. Give the speakers a prompt and let the talking begin. After approximately ninety seconds, have one of the circles move one or two people to the right (or left). Change the speaker to the listener. Offer another prompt for speaking. Continue this process as needed (usually three or four times).

Gallery Walks

Decide on the critical attributes of the content and write each attribute on a single sheet of chart paper and display them around the room. (Optional: use photos or art work about the content.)

On each piece of chart paper write a prompt for students to perform a task or write their thoughts, questions, or insights.

Organize students into groups and assign each group a poster as their starting point for the gallery walk.

Have groups complete their task on the chart paper and then move to the next poster. (Option: at each new poster, have students hand the marker to a new group member.)

Mimes

Have the students watch a mime, perhaps from YouTube or Vimeo.

Review the learning targets for the unit.

Move students into small groups in order to prepare a mime that reflects one learning target.

Have groups perform their mimes.

During the presentations, other group members write their interpretation of the presentation and share at the end of the performance.

Music, Movement, and Musing

Gather enough four-by-six-inch cards so that each student in the classroom has his/her own card.

Write a significant element from the content of the unit on each card (for example, vocabulary words, major concepts, key sentences from the reading, pictures related to the content, problems from the math or science content, a quote that connects to the content).

Give each student a card.

Turn the music on and ask students to move around the room exchanging cards.

Stop the music and have students pair up with the last person they exchanged a card with. Their task is to talk about, define, or solve whatever is on the card.

Have the students exchange cards.

Start the music again and continue the process.

Be sure to model this activity in advance with a small group of students

Silent Chalk Talk

Make sure you have a large number of markers for this activity.

On the board or chart paper, write a topic or question for the students to think about. (If you are using chart paper, you will need multiple pieces of the paper.) Distribute the multiple markers along the board or chart paper.

Ask students to come stand in front of the board or chart paper.

Explain that they will engage in a silent conversation by writing on the chart paper or board questions or comments about the topic or question. They may respond to comments by other students or draw lines between comments that show the connection of ideas.

Tell them that you will inform them when the silent chalk talk is over so from the time that you say, "Silent Chalk Talk begins" to the time that you say, "Silent Chalk Talk is over," they are absolutely not to talk but to write on the chart paper/board.

Begin the chalk talk and continue for as long as their energy in the room.

Be sure to debrief.

Works Cited

Achebe, C. 1994. *Things Fall Apart*. New York: Anchor Books.

Beers, K., R. E. Probst, and L. Rief, eds. 2007. *Adolescent Literacy: Turning Promise into Practice*. Portsmouth, NH: Heinemann.

Bennett, S. 2007. *That Workshop Book: New Systems and Structures for Classrooms That Read, Write, and Think*. Portsmouth, NH: Heinemann.

Black, P., W. Dylan, and C. Harrison. 2003. *Assessment for Learning*. New York: Open University Press.

Blankstein, A. M. 2004. *Failure Is Not an Option: Six Principles That Guide Student Achievement in High-Performing Schools*. Thousand Oaks, CA: Corwin Press.

Boyne, J. 2006. *The Boy in the Striped Pajamas*. New York: Random House.

Calkins, L. 2012. *Pathways to the Common Core: Accelerating Achievement*. Portsmouth, NH: Heinemann.

Chappuis, J. 2009. *Seven Strategies of Assessment for Learning*. Boston: Pearson.

Chiu, M. M. 2008. "Flowing Toward Correct Contributions During Group Problem Solving: A Statistical Discourse Analysis." *Journal of the Learning Sciences* 17: 415–463.

Coalition of Essential Schools. The CES Common Principles. www.essentialschools.org/items/4.

Common Core State Standards Initiative. 2010. www.corestandards.org/assets/CCSSI_ELA%20Standards.pdf.

———. 2012a. Application for English Learners. www.corestandards.org/assets/application-for-english-learners.pdf.

———. 2012b. Application to Students with Disabilities. www.corestandards.org/assets/application-to-students-with-disabilities.pdf.

Csikszentmihalyi, M. 1997. *Finding Flow: The Psychology of Engagement with Everyday Life*. New York: Basic Books.

———. 1990 and 2008. *Flow: The Psychology of Optimal Experience*. New York: Harper Collins.

Dalton, S. 2007. *Five Standards for Effective Teaching*. San Francisco: Jossey-Bass.

EPE Research Center. 2007. EPE Research Center. *Diplomas Count*. Education Week. Bethusda, MD.

Dweck, C. S. 2006. *Mindset: The New Psychology of Success*. New York: Random House.

———. 2007. "The Praise a Child Should Never Hear." February 13, 2007.

———. 2012. Keynote address at Learning Forward Summer Conference, July, Denver, Colorado.

ESPN. 2010. "The Wizard's Wisdom: 'Woodenisms.'" Originally published June 4, 2010. http://sports.espn.go.com/ncb/news/story?id=5249709.

Facione, P. A. 2011. *Critical Thinking: What It Is and Why It Counts*. Milbrae, CA: Insight Assessment.

Freire, P., and D. P. Macedo. 1987. *Literacy: Reading the Word and the World.* Westport, CT: Bergin and Garvey.

Frey, N., D. Fisher, and S. Everlove. 2009. *Productive Group Work: How to Engage Students, Build Teamwork, and Promote Understanding.* Alexandria, VA: ASCD.

Galeano, E. 1992. *The Book of Embraces.* New York: Norton Press.

Gardner, H. 2006. *Multiple Intelligences: New Horizons in Theory and Practice*, 2nd Ed. New York: Basic Books.

Gay, G. 2000. *Culturally Responsive Teaching: Theory, Research, and Practice.* New York: Teachers College Press.

Gonzalez, N., L. Moll, and C. Amanti. 2005. *Funds of Knowledge: Theorizing Practices in Households and Classrooms.* Abingdon, United Kingdom: Lawrence Erlbaum Associates.

Gregory, A., R. J. Skiba, and P. A. Noguera. 2010. "The Achievement Gap and the Discipline Gap: Two Sides of the Same Coin?" *Educational Researcher* 39: 59–68.

Hattie, J. 2012a. "Know Thy Impact." *Education Leadership* 70: 18–23.

———. 2012b. *Visible Learning for Teachers: Maximizing Impact on Learning.* New York: Routledge.

Heacox, D. 2009. *Making Differentiation a Habit: How to Ensure Success in Academically Diverse Classrooms.* Minneapolis, MN: Free Spirit Publishing.

Himmele, P., and W. Himmele. 2011. *Total Participation Techniques: Making Every Student an Active Learner.* Alexandria, VA: ASCD.

Howard, G. 2006. *We Can't Teach What We Don't Know.* New York: Teachers College Press.

Jacobs, J. 2008. "What Is Rigor?" Blog entry, October 30. Available at Linking and Thinking on Education. www.joannejacobs.com/2008/10/what-is-rigor/.

Johnston, P. H. 2004. *Choice Words: How Our Language Affects Children's Learning.* Portland, ME: Stenhouse.

———. 2012. *Opening Minds: Using Language to Change Lives.* Portland, ME: Stenhouse.

King, S., and A. Watson. 2010. "Teaching Excellence for All Our Students" *Theory into Practice* 49: 3, 178.

Kinney, J. 2007. *Diary of a Wimpy Kid.* New York: Abrams.

Kirby, D., and D. L. Kirby. 2007. *New Directions in Teaching Memoir: A Studio Workshop Approach.* Portsmouth, NH: Heinemann.

Lewis, H. 2012. "Reinventing the Classroom: Anatomy of a New Course—and a New Approach to Teaching It." *Harvard Magazine* (September/October): 54–57.

Lovelace, T. 2012. "Does the Common Core Matter?" *Education Week* (April): 32.

Martino, S. 2012. "The Impact of Flexible Grouping on Mathematical Understanding of Heterogeneous Math Classes." Unpublished master's thesis, Colorado State University.

Marzano, R., and D. Pickering. 2011. *The Highly Engaged Classroom.* Bloomington, IN: Marzano Research Lab.

Massimini, F., and M. Carli. 1988. "The Systematic Assessment of Flow in Daily Experience." In *Optional Experience: Psychological Studies of Flow in Consciousness*, edited by M. Csikszentmihalyi and I. S. Csikszentmihalyi. New York: Cambridge University Press. 266–287.

Mehan, H. 1979. *Learning Lessons.* Cambridge, MA: Harvard University Press.

Middleton, M. J. 2009. "Academic Press." In *Psychology of Classroom Learning: An Encyclopedia,* ed. E. Anderman. Detroit: Macmillan Reference.

Moll, L., C. Amanti, D. Neff, and N. Gonzalez. 2001. "Funds of Knowledge for Teaching: Using a Qualitative Approach to Connect Homes and Classrooms." *Theory into Practice,* 31 (2): 132–141.

Moroney, B. 2013. "The Praise a Child Should Never Hear." *Wall Street Journal.* (March 28). Available at Informed Reader. http://blogs.wsj.com/informedreader/2007/02/13/the-praise-a-child-should-never-hear/.

National Research Council. 2004. *Engaging Schools: Fostering High School Students' Motivation to Learn.* Washington, DC: National Academies Press.

Newmann, F. M., ed. 1992. *Student Engagement and Achievement in American Schools.* New York: Teachers College Press.

Nuthall, G. 2005. *The Cultural Myths and Realities of Classroom Teaching and Learning: A Personal Journey.* New York: Teachers College Press.

Nystrand, M. 1997. *Opening Dialogue: Understanding the Dynamics of Language and Learning in the English Classroom.* New York: Teachers College Press.

OnlineCollege.org website. 2010. "Fifty Famously Successful People Who Failed at First." www.onlinecollege.org/2010/02/16/50-famously-successful-people-who-failed-at-first/.

Partnership for 21st Century Skills. "A Framework for 21st Century Learning." www.p21.org.

Paul, R., and L. Elder. 2006. *Critical Thinking: Tools for Taking Charge of Your Learning and Your Life.* Upper Saddle Hill, NJ: Pearson Prentice Hall.

Peck, S. 1998. *The Different Drum: Community-Making and Peace.* New York: Touchstone Press.

Pink, D. 2009. *Drive: The Surprising Truth about What Motivates Us.* New York: Riverhead Books.

Quate, S. 2012. "A Critical Incident." Thinking About Life blog, April 3. http://stevi-steviq.blogspot.com/.

Quate, S., and J. McDermott. 2009. *Clock Watchers: Six Steps to Motivating and Engaging Disengaged Students Across Content Areas.* Portsmouth, NH: Heinemann.

Resnick, L. 1987. *Education and Learning to Think.* Washington, DC: National Academy Press.

Richardson, J. 2000. Presentation at Cherry Creek School District, Aurora, Colorado.

Schunk, D. H., P. R. Pintrich, and J. L. Meece. 2008. *Motivation in Education.* 3rd ed. Columbus, OH: Pearson.

Shouse, R. C. 1996. "Academic Press and Sense of Community: Conflict and Congruence in American High Schools." *Research in Sociology of Education and Socialization* 11: 173–202.

Sizer, T. 2004. *Horace's Compromise: The Dilemma of American High School.* New York: Houghton-Mifflin.

Smith, F. 1987. *Joining the Literacy Club: Further Essays into Education*. Portsmouth, NH: Heinemann.

Smith, M., and J. Wilhelm. 2006. *Going with the Flow: How to Engage Boys (and Girls) in Their Literacy Learning*. Portsmouth, NH: Heinemann.

Sousa, D. 2011. *How The Brain Learns*. Thousand Oaks, CA: Corwin Press.

Stanovich, K. 1986. "Matthew Effects in Reading: Some Consequences of Individual Differences." *Reading Research Quarterly* 21 (Fall): 360–406.

Strong, R., H. Silver, and M. Perini. 2001. *Teaching What Matters Most: Standards and Strategies for Raising Student Achievement*. Alexandria, VA: ASCD.

Tharp, R., and R. Gallimore. 1988. *Rousing Minds to Life*. Cambridge, UK: Cambridge University Press.

Tharp, R., P. Estrada, S. Dalton, and L. Yamauchi. 2001. *Teaching Transformed: Achieving Excellence, Fairness, Inclusion, and Harmony*. Boulder, CO: Westview Press.

Tomlinson, C. A. 2004. "The Mobius Effect: Addressing Learner Variance in Schools." *Journal of Learning Disabilities* 37 (6): 516–524.

Tomlinson, C. A., and M. Imbeau. 2011. *Leading and Managing a Differentiated Classroom*. Alexandria, VA: ASCD.

Tomlinson, C. A., and E. L. Javius. 2012. "Teach Up for Leadership." *Education Leadership* 69 (February): 28–33.

Tovani, C. 2000. *I Read It, But I Don't Get It: Comprehension Strategies for Adolescent Readers*. Portland, ME: Stenhouse.

———. 2004. *Do I Really Have to Teach Reading?* Portland, ME: Stenhouse.

Vitto, J. 2003. *Relationship Driven Classroom Management: Strategies That Promote Student Motivation*. Thousand Oaks, CA: Corwin Press.

Vygotsky, L. S. 1989. *Thought and Language*. Cambridge, MA: MIT Press.

Wells, G., and G. L. Chang-Wells. 1992. *Constructing Knowledge Together: Classrooms as Centers of Inquiry and Literacy*. Portsmouth, NH: Heinemann.

Wiggins, G., and J. McTighe. 2005. *Understanding by Design*. Alexandria, VA: ASCD.

Wilhelm, J. 2007. *Engaging Readers & Writers with Inquiry*. New York: Scholastic.

Wink, J. 2011. *Critical Pedagogy*. Boston: Pearson.

Yu Hua. 2003. *To Live*. Trans. M. Berry. New York: Anchor Books.

Index

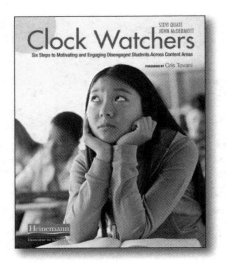